Kika & Me

Dr Amit Patel is a disability rights campaigner, fundraiser, motivational speaker and independent diversity and accessibility consultant. He studied medicine at Cambridge University and qualified as a doctor, specializing in emergency medicine and major incidents. During medical school Amit was diagnosed with keratoconus, an eye condition that is usually easily treated with a corneal transplant. However, he was one of the rare individuals for whom the transplants rejected and he was registered severely sight impaired (blind) in 2013, just one year after getting married. After coming to terms with his own sight loss, Amit set out to help others who were new to sight loss, through volunteering with the Royal National Institute of Blind People and the Guide Dogs for the Blind Association. Amit is married to Seema and they have two children. *Kika & Me* is his first book.

Kika is a white Labrador who has been matched to Amit since September 2015.

You can follow Amit and Kika's adventures on Twitter @BlindDad_Uk and @Kika_GuideDog, and on Instagram @kika_guidedo~

Dr Amit Patel

with Chris Manby

Kika & Me

*How one extraordinary guide dog
changed my world*

PAN BOOKS

First published 2020 by Macmillan

This paperback edition first published 2021 by Pan Books
an imprint of Pan Macmillan
The Smithson, 6 Briset Street, London EC1M 5NR
EU representative: Macmillan Publishers Ireland
Limited, Mallard Lodge, Lansdowne Village, Dublin 4
Associated companies throughout the world
www.panmacmillan.com

ISBN 978-1-5290-2123-3

1 3 5 7 9 8 6 4 2

A CIP catalogue record for this book is available from the British Library.

Typeset by Palimpsest Book Production Ltd, Falkirk, Stirlingshire
Printed and bound by CPI Group (UK) Ltd, Croydon, CR0 4YY

Visit **www.panmacmillan.com** to read more about all our books
and to buy them. You will also find features, author interviews and
news of any author events, and you can sign up for e-newsletters
so that you're always first to hear about our new releases.

To my beautiful wife Seema: without your belief in us
I would have never found my way when the lights
suddenly went out.

To Kika, Abhishek and Anoushka:
I'm a better person because of you.

Contents

Prologue

Rush hour on the London Underground is not for the faint-hearted. As thousands of people descend on the busiest stations at the end of the working day, it's easy to feel intimidated by the crush of humanity intent on getting home, just as I was one winter afternoon in 2014. But making it even more overwhelming for me was the fact that, just a year earlier, I had lost my sight.

It had been a long day. In the morning, I'd set out towards central London with a tentative spring in my step to attend a Living with Sight Loss course at the Royal National Institute of Blind People (RNIB). I'd recently learned to use a white cane and I knew the journey well. After a slight mishap on my first trip, I'd memorized the route with precision. I knew exactly where I needed to be on the Tube to make sure I got out at the right end of the platform at King's Cross and found the steps that would take me to the exit closest to the RNIB offices.

Though it was a journey I'd done several times by this point, I still found getting from A to B with my white cane tiring. Arriving in the room where the course took place, I would collapse into a chair and gratefully accept the offer of a coffee. I always needed it. All the people I'd met on the course so far felt the same way when they arrived. There was great camaraderie in our shared stories of the trials of travelling across the city while blind.

Because the journey to the RNIB took so much out of me, I was careful to minimize the potential for problems on the way home. That meant I usually left the office when the Tube was least likely to be busy. I'd worked out that I needed to be on my way before three o'clock, which marked kick-out time for the kids at the local secondary schools.

But on that particular day, I did not leave the office before three. I enjoyed being at the RNIB, talking to people who knew what it was like to navigate a world without sight. It was a real relief to be able to chat about the ups and downs of my life, knowing that my new friends understood every single thing I was saying. I don't remember what we were talking about on that occasion, but it was interesting enough to make me decide that it wouldn't hurt to hang on for a little longer than usual. I was reluctant to bring the conversation to a close.

Eventually, the group began to break up and we went our separate ways. I said a cheerful goodbye to my friends and the course leader and headed for King's Cross. I retraced the steps I'd made that morning, crossed the big main road, found the right entrance to the station and took the escalator down to the Tube. I wondered as I did so whether I would ever really get used to travelling on the Underground again. Working as an A&E doctor near King's Cross before I lost my sight, my daily journey to and from work had held very few surprises, but without sight the Underground was a different world.

That winter day I had misjudged my departure time badly, getting to the station at the moment when the school run met the beginning of rush hour proper. The tunnels down to the platform echoed with the voices of excited teenagers, playing out their little dramas at full volume.

Ordinarily, on getting to the platform, I would have stayed close to the spot where I entered, knowing that I would be in line with a train door when the Tube came in. That day it was too busy to stand where I wanted to. People were pouring down the escalator behind me and I was jostled and shoved as they tried to squeeze onto the platform. I hated being knocked into so I decided I would move along to try to find just a little more room. Getting through the crowd was hard work. Once London commuters have found their spot, they stick to it. Absorbed in their phones and their newspapers, they probably didn't even notice my cane. But I persevered and after a while the crowd did thin out. I felt a little easier. I breathed deeply and tried to relax. I hoped I wouldn't have to wait too long. There had been no announcement of a delay.

An underground tunnel is an echo chamber to me. The shape of the walls and the ceramic tiles bounce noise all around. It wasn't something I noticed when I could still see, but now the soundscape was so much more important to me, I found it difficult to ignore the cacophony. Unable to tell where noises were coming from because of all the conflicting echoes, I didn't hear *him* approaching me.

The first thing I knew was that someone had grabbed me by the tops of my arms. What was going on? Were they trying to stop me from getting too close to the platform edge? Were they trying to help? No. That wasn't it. They weren't pulling me back – they were turning me around. I guessed from the height and the strength that the person holding me was male. Young. Strong. He turned me easily, though when he spoke I realized he could only be a teenager.

He spun me round and round and then he said, with a confident sneer in his voice, 'Let's see if you can find your way now.'

Then he let go of my arms and just carried on down the platform. In his wake went more teens, both male and female, laughing at his daring, congratulating him on his great joke. But it was no joke to me.

Moments earlier, I'd been waiting calmly for my train. Being on such a busy platform wasn't ideal but at least I'd known roughly where I was. I'd estimated that I was a good distance from the edge, with my back to the tunnel wall, facing the train tracks. The safest position. Now I had no idea where I was at all.

I felt right then as though I was absolutely alone on that platform. I could hear only the sound of my blood in my head as a sense of panic began to engulf me. I could not move. I didn't dare. It was too dangerous. If I stepped in the wrong direction, towards the tracks, I could be stepping straight into oblivion.

Had no one else seen what had happened? Nobody was coming to my aid. I would have asked for help but my voice had frozen in my throat and I could only croak. I felt the prickle of shame and embarrassment behind my eyes and beneath my armpits as I grew hotter and hotter and came close to tears.

In the middle of rush hour at one of London's busiest

stations, surrounded by my fellow commuters, I felt like I was on my own in hell. I'd been pranked by a bunch of kids but their joke, which would be forgotten by the time they were home, had left me fearing for my life, literally not knowing where to turn as the next train thundered down the track.

1

The Wild Child

I grew up in the eighties in the town of Guildford in the south-east of England, with my parents and my little brother Mital. I had a very happy childhood. Our family was tight knit and endlessly supportive. Mum and Dad were always there for us. Their marriage was the rock-solid base from which Mital and I could venture out into the world with confidence.

Having moved to Guildford from Croydon, Mum and Dad bought a corner shop, which soon became a staple for their new neighbours. It allowed us to meet all the residents as they popped in for their daily supplies. Even today, when I walk down the streets of Guildford I always run into someone who remembers me as a child and they always ask after my parents and my brother. Family and community were the pillars of our life.

My parents' love gave me the belief I could do anything. That 'anything' changed from week to week. One day I wanted to be an Olympic skier, the next a world-class cricketer, the next a Formula One star. I had a lot of energy and sport was my passion. Any kind would do. Mum and Dad's loft is still packed with the evidence of my short-lived enthusiasms for everything from skating to football. I was fortunate that my secondary school, the Bishop Reindorp School, was perfectly set up for someone as sport-crazy as me. Though it wasn't fee-paying or private, it had amazing sports facilities, including proper football pitches and a dry ski slope. There weren't many schools in England where you could learn skiing in PE.

Outside school, I loved to go rollerblading with my mates in the Tesco car park, dreaming of one day being a speed-skating champion. When the Spectrum ice rink opened up in Guildford, I took the skills I'd learned rollerblading and transferred them to ice hockey, imagining myself as a professional hockey star. I also played table tennis for the county.

When I turned fourteen, I persuaded Dad to teach me to drive on a local disused runway. I couldn't wait to get my licence. I was born to be a boy racer – in my head, Dad's Nissan Primera was a Formula One car – but Dad reined me in with his usual patience, reminding me that I wouldn't pass my test by breaking speed limits.

Around the same time, I clubbed together with two school-mates to buy a clapped-out old motorbike from our PE teacher. When I brought it home and asked to keep it in our garage, Mum and Dad weren't best pleased, but they indulged me, as they had through every other Amit craze. I think they thought that fixing the bike would keep me out of trouble for a bit. I didn't tell them I'd already nearly driven the bike into a pond, with my two friends on the back, while trying it out in the local park.

Yes, as a kid, I was on the go all the time. I was easily bored. My school teachers were patient, but if there was a distraction from schoolwork to be had, I was all over it.

I always wanted to try new things. I had to be told to sit down and shut up several times a day. However, while I was often distracted, I was lucky that I also found it easy to study when I really had to. Science and maths did interest me and I only had to read something once or twice for it to stick. This meant I could get through exams without too much effort and, so long as I was getting good grades, my wilder exploits went largely unnoticed.

There was, however, one area of school life where I had to have discipline. That was in the ATC – the Air Training Corps. I joined the local squadron, which was led by Warrant Officer Wachtel, because on top of everything else I'd always wanted to fly. Warrant Officer Wachtel was pretty scary and didn't have to ask anyone to do something twice. Regardless, he also had the respect of everyone who encountered him. He was fair and taught me that discipline was about more than endlessly polishing your boots. Though there was an awful lot of polishing boots . . . Years later, I would realize just how valuable the lessons Warrant Officer Wachtel instilled in me really were.

Back in the classroom we talked about choosing a career. When it came to me, it was obvious that I would never be the kind to feel content behind a desk. When I joined the ATC I thought the Air Force might be an option. I knew I wouldn't be able to be a fighter pilot – my ultimate dream job – because I wore glasses, but I hoped there would be another interesting role that would take me up in the air and around the world.

Whenever there was an opportunity, I went up in an aeroplane. I just loved the feeling of freedom I got from being in the air. With the ATC, I learned to pilot a simple training plane called a Chipmunk. The ATC also had a flight simulator, modelled on the cockpit of a fighter jet. It didn't work but I spent many happy hours trying to fix it. My theory was that you had to take something apart to properly understand it. I was very good at taking things apart. I wasn't always so successful at putting them back together.

I may not have got to fly a jet for real, but after I finished my GCSEs, my friends and I saved up to celebrate with a parachute jump. Nothing made me happier than the adrenalin high of a calculated risk. If there was an adventure to be had, I was up for it. There was no scheme too mad, too wild or too dangerous. I was determined to live my life to the full.

I had planned to travel around the world after I finished my A levels, but when I was offered a place at Cambridge University to read medicine that autumn, I knew there was no way I could turn it down. It was a big deal to get an offer from such a prestigious establishment and Mum and Dad were of course over the moon. So, at the age of eighteen, I went straight from school to university. I was excited. It wasn't the round-the-world trip I'd been looking forward to, but I knew it would be an adventure of a different kind.

Being at Cambridge was a culture shock in many ways. I was just an ordinary kid from boringly middle-class Guildford. Cambridge is a place where the very walls seem to breathe tradition, exclusivity and privilege. The college I lived in felt like being in a stately home. The black-tie dinners with seven kinds of cutlery and the exclusive male-only clubs were too fancy for me. However, I soon found a good group of friends who made my university experience great fun as we bonded over our shared enthusiasms.

True to form, during my first term, I spent a lot of time when I should have been in the library studying playing various sports. My new friends introduced me to golf and I was soon hooked, deciding as I always did that I had to master this new skill to the highest possible level. I could never do anything by halves. That said, often we didn't make it out onto the course because we were having too much fun in the clubhouse. I also joined the local flying club so that I could keep flying and gliding.

During the long holidays, I went back to Guildford and worked shifts in Mum and Dad's shop with my textbooks spread out over the counter. The regular customers seemed as keen as my family that I should succeed. One year, when my parents were visiting family in India, leaving my brother and me in charge, one very kind retired lady customer even offered to watch the shop while I revised.

As the years progressed, I had very little time to do anything but study, but I was happy. I got through my three pre-med years and moved on to my 'rotations', where I had to spend time in a different hospital department every couple of months. It's while on rotation that trainee doctors decide in which area of medicine they'd like to specialize. When it came to my turn, I was based at Addenbrooke's, Cambridge University's famous teaching hospital.

I was slightly nervous as I began this crucial part of my training and came face to face with real patients for the first time. There were many moments when I found myself wondering what on earth I was supposed to do. I worked under the watch of some seriously scary old-school matrons, but they were always quick to offer help, advice and reassurance to this newbie and to make me feel a part of the NHS family. There were also some real highs, such as when I delivered a baby for the first time.

I worked hard but I'm sure I must have been a frustration to the brilliant consultants I encountered at Addenbrooke's because even then, as a young adult, I still wanted to do things my own way. I was young and idealistic and had hundreds of ideas as to how things could be better. In the under-resourced NHS, it felt as though nobody had enough time. The sort of pastoral care that patients needed fell by the wayside when there were treatment targets to be met. I found that hard to understand when it seemed obvious that the psychological well-being of patients was every bit as important as giving them the right drugs. Happier people got better more quickly, was the way I saw it.

My parents had raised me to do whatever I could to help people who needed it, and once I was in a hospital environment I found it difficult to switch that off. Many of the patients I met had no family to visit them and no one to talk to. As a result, I'd spend much longer with them than I was supposed to and when I finished a shift I would often go back to check on a patient I had attended earlier in the day. That doubled an already heavy workload. But the way I'd grown up had convinced me that community was paramount and I firmly believed that everybody was important enough for a piece of my time.

It wasn't just the patients who were getting the short end of the stick thanks to pressure on resources. A few of the senior doctors I met treated the nurses dismissively, but I soon learned that it's the nurses who really run the hospital and their experience deserves enormous respect. I know I wouldn't have got through my time at Addenbrooke's without their support.

The rotations were tough to say the least. Having endured ridiculously long anti-social working hours as junior doctors, many of my friends from medical school understandably chose specialisms that would allow them to have a semblance of a 'normal' life, with a nine-to-five working routine. Me? Well, I plumped for the very opposite. I knew that I wanted to be a trauma specialist. My friends thought I was nuts but I just loved the craziness. I loved having to think on my feet. I loved being hands on. It was the perfect discipline for me – the kid who needed constant excitement to feel truly alive. In A&E, no two days were ever the same, but almost every shift had a moment that gave me an adrenalin high like jumping out of an aeroplane at 13,000 feet.

I was soon offered a role in London, but before starting it, I volunteered for six months in India with the Red Cross. I started out near Mumbai and worked my way to the north of India as part of a team that travelled from village to village offering routine checks and vaccinations to those who didn't have access to regular healthcare. We ran classes for children on the importance of hygiene and delivered the occasional baby too.

At the end of that stint, when my brother Mital met me at the airport, he wasn't in the least bit surprised to find me dressed in shorts, flip-flops and a T-shirt despite the bitterly cold British weather. I'd left all my other clothes with the people I'd been living with, figuring they needed them more than I did. I'd also grown a big bushy beard.

'I'm not even walking with you,' Mital said as we headed to his car.

I wanted to be of service to those less fortunate than me whenever I could be. In 2004, I managed to take a week out of work in A&E and flew out to Asia in the wake of the Boxing Day tsunami. The tsunami itself killed almost 250,000 people, but that was just the beginning of the horror. The devastation it left in its wake provided the perfect environment for diseases such as cholera to thrive. I joined a relief team and did my best to be useful, providing check-ups and vaccinations.

Growing up, the Indian way of life had a big influence on me. I was raised a Hindu. Our family was part of a large community. I knew all my aunts and uncles and spent many happy weekends with my cousins. We went to the temple over an hour away in Wembley most Sundays. Even though I went to a Church of England school (and for a while also went to Sunday school!) my parents ensured I didn't forget my culture and religion.

Since Mum was from Mumbai and Dad from Gujarat, I also went on many trips to India as a child. I was about six years old when I went on my first trip. My maternal grandmother was a headmistress in Madhya Pradesh and when we stayed with her we also visited the school where she taught. The difference between the resources available to my grandmother's pupils and what I had back home was astonishing. The school in Madhya Pradesh was a simple village school

– it was basic in its provisions – but the pupils were always immaculately turned out in their blue and white uniforms. They were also very keen to learn. Whenever we visited, we would take with us pens, colouring pencils and notebooks. My grandmother's students were always excited to get new school equipment in a way that I rarely was! I undoubtedly lived a privileged life back home in Guildford, but it was in India that I learned you can find true happiness whatever your circumstances. The generosity and stoicism of the people I met in Madhya Pradesh was humbling. The people who had the least were inevitably the most generous with what they did have.

After the experiences I'd had while volunteering and spending time with my family in India, I was still ambitious, but not for money or other obvious signs of status. I knew I didn't need to be rich to feel that I was succeeding in life. I didn't need swanky watches and fancy cars. Success to me was putting a smile on someone's face. It was making someone's life better. I still felt working in A&E would be the perfect fit with my life goals. Everything was falling into place.

2

Second Chances

It was while I was studying medicine that I first learned I had an eye condition called keratoconus. It's a progressive eye disease in which the cornea – the transparent front part of the eye which covers the iris and pupil, and which is normally round – starts to become cone-like in shape. This means that it can no longer accurately focus light onto the retina at the back of the eye and when this happens, your vision is distorted and blurred.

Keratoconus is normally picked up in childhood during routine eye tests. I don't know why that wasn't the case for me. As a child, I'd definitely had a lot of them. I'd worn glasses for short-sightedness since the age of eight. My first pair had bright blue rims chosen to match my school uniform. I remember how proud I was when the teacher called me to the front of the class so I could show my classmates my flashy new specs.

Throughout my school days, my prescription didn't change much. Certainly not enough to raise alarm. As you've already seen, wearing glasses didn't stop me from doing anything I wanted. I faced down cricket balls. I skied. I skated like a madman on wheels and on ice. I even jumped out of planes. My specs were just a minor inconvenience. However, while

I was at medical school, I started to get migraines for the first time in my life.

When the headaches began, I assumed it must be because I was constantly reading, studying late into the night as I worked hard to ace my exams. But when a change of lens prescription didn't seem to make any difference, I forked out to see a private optician for a second opinion. I was astonished when keratoconus was diagnosed. Though I was a medical student, it wasn't a condition I knew all that much about at the time. I set about educating myself at once. Keratoconus affects around one in 450 people. Thankfully, though, it doesn't inevitably lead to blindness. The private optician told me it could be controlled with special lenses that would push my cornea back into the correct shape so that light could be properly focused on my retina again. The only problem was, it would take a while to get hold of those lenses. Maybe a couple of months.

Right then, time was the one thing I didn't have. I was coming up to my final exams and I needed to get through them. After five years of working my socks off, I couldn't afford to fail now. So right after I got my diagnosis, I called the eye clinic back home at the Royal Surrey Hospital. I was fortunate that the consultant there understood at once how important it was for me to be able to do my exams, which were just a month away. Though he couldn't fit me in at his clinic, he was kind enough to invite me to his house, where we spent three hours in his office experimenting with sample lenses that might get me through the next few crucial weeks. Thankfully, we found a pair that would work.

The first set of lenses the consultant gave me were like

half-size contact lenses – though slightly harder – with a dip in the middle to literally push my corneas back into shape. He warned me that they would have to be changed every few months as the shape of my eye continued to deteriorate, which was, he explained, almost inevitable. It was all about managing the condition. However, blindness wasn't mentioned.

The lenses were uncomfortable and difficult to wear – they felt heavy and were sharp and scratchy, especially when they slipped behind my eyes – but with their help I got through those crucial exams.

Unfortunately, it wasn't long before the emergency lenses were no longer sitting properly on my eyes, just as the consultant had predicted. I needed larger lenses. I got larger lenses. And then larger lenses again. Over the next couple of years, as I worked as a junior doctor in a busy London A&E department, my corneas became so misshapen that the lenses I had to wear were like miniature glass pasta bowls that covered the whole of the front of my eyeball. What's more, they had to be filled with a saline solution before they could be placed over the eye.

Putting them in was a real hassle. If any of the liquid spilled out before I could get a lens into place, I would end up with a bubble in my vision. As it was, even if I got the lenses in correctly without spilling a drop, during the day they would always leak fluid so that by the end of a shift at the hospital I had a visible tideline across my eye. I could tell that some of my patients noticed it as I was examining them. It must have looked pretty odd. If I thought the patient could take it, or that it might helpfully distract them from their pain,

I would invite them to tap on my eyeball, which, while the lens was in, felt like a glass eye. It would either put them at ease or completely freak them out!

But sadly, after a while, even the enormous pasta bowl lenses weren't working to keep my corneas in shape, and I knew something really drastic needed to be done. It was agreed that as soon as I was able to take the time off, I would have a corneal transplant – an operation to remove my damaged corneas and replace them with healthy donor tissue.

It was a serious undertaking with many risks, including rejection, where your immune system recognizes that the donated cornea does not belong to you and attacks it. Other potential side-effects included astigmatism, glaucoma and retinal detachment. There was also the chance that the keratoconus could come back. For that reason, I couldn't have both eyes operated on at once. My consultant decided that my right eye should be done first and that the operation should take place at the Royal Surrey Hospital so that I would be near home. I'd be staying with Mum and Dad as I recovered.

Though I'd been nervous beforehand, the transplant went really well. At first my vision was a little blurry and I had to use steroid drops, but eventually my right eye cleared and I had perfect sight again. At least on that side.

The redness cleared after a week and I was able to go back to work within three. I can't tell you what a relief it was to no longer have to wear the awful glass lens on my right eye. The only evidence that I'd had an operation at all was that if you looked at my eye from a certain angle, you could see tiny blue stitches.

Three to four months later, once my right eye was properly settled, my consultant decided it was time to do my left. Unfortunately, the operation didn't go quite so smoothly this time. For some reason, there was a crease in the transplanted cornea, which carried with it a chance of infection. However, three to four weeks into my recovery, despite the crease, all seemed to be going well. I could see again without using any lenses to keep my corneas in shape at all. Though I did still need to wear glasses, you can't imagine how much easier it made my day-to-day life. I went back to work at the hospital feeling invincible. After a couple of years spent faffing about with those unwieldy liquid-filled glass lenses, I could forget about my eyes at last.

I was enormously grateful to the people whose donated corneas had made it possible and resolved to make the most of their gift. I thought about them a lot – who they'd been and what their lives had been like. Through the generous decision they'd made in their lifetimes to be donors, I'd been given a second chance.

Six months later, though, I felt the familiar pangs of pain again. The headaches began anew and my eyes started to look angry and red. For a while I tried to keep going with steroid drops, but soon they weren't keeping the inflammation down and I couldn't keep pretending that nothing was going on. At the eye clinic, the consultant confirmed the bad news: my left corneal transplant was rejecting and needed to be replaced as soon as possible. I couldn't believe it: my body wasn't accepting the donated cornea and my right eye was over-compensating and feeling the pain too.

It was not the news I wanted, but at the same time I knew,

because of my medical training, that it didn't have to be a total disaster. It had been made clear to me from the start there was a risk that, because of the crease, the left lens would eventually become infected and have to be removed. I told myself that a new corneal transplant would take that risk off the table. It was worth going through the operation again for the peace of mind. It had made such a difference to my right eye after all.

I had no idea at that point that over the next few years, I would have another five transplants, between both eyes, in quick succession. Rejection in one eye would slowly start a chain reaction in the other eye and, like a merry-go-round, so it went on. No one could tell me why I experienced so many transplant rejections, though one theory was that I had an overactive immune system. By the time I got to number seven, I was warned by my consultant that I was becoming too high-risk for another operation should anything go wrong again. All I could do was cross my fingers and pray that this transplant would prove to be a lucky seventh.

For a while, it did feel as though my luck was holding. Everything seemed OK. I got on with my day-to-day life with no lenses and clear vision. I was enjoying my job in A&E. I'd bought a house of my own in Guildford. Then, almost two years after that seventh transplant, it started all over again. My eyes were bright red and painful even when I hadn't been at work all day. Sometimes it was as though I was looking at the world through frosted glass. Though I did my best to soldier on for a couple of weeks, I knew the signs of transplant rejection only too well.

This time, however, I wasn't calm about it at all. Knowing

that the NHS would not put me forward for another op, I was desperate. I couldn't bear the thought that there really was nothing to be done to save my sight this time. I wasn't even thirty yet. I wouldn't accept it.

Once it was confirmed by a consultant that transplant seven was rejecting, I called Dad and told him I wanted to go to the States to see what could be done there. I had old friends from university who were working in America and they'd spoken of pioneering treatments that weren't yet possible in the UK. The treatments were experimental and full of the associated risks, but I was ready to be a guinea pig. I would consider *anything*. My parents were right behind me. They swung into action again.

I had an uncle – Dad's cousin, Pradip – in New Jersey. Over the years, Pradip has been like a second father to me. He immediately agreed that Dad and I should fly out and stay with him and his family while we investigated the options Stateside. I explained the situation to my bosses at work, then packed a suitcase with a couple of days' worth of clothes and a ridiculous number of single-use vials of anti-inflammatory eye drops.

The flight was tense. I was in pain and spent a lot of time crying. Dad did his best to keep me optimistic but he was anxious on my behalf. I knew that travelling so far to find help was a long shot. But within days of finding out that I was losing that precious seventh cornea, I was sitting across a desk from an eye specialist in New York.

America has a reputation for going bigger and better in everything and corneal transplants were no exception to this rule. My university friends were right. In the US, they were trialling solutions I couldn't even have imagined. Forget about transplanting human corneas. That was old hat. The first specialist I spoke to suggested taking the rejecting corneas out using a laser and replacing them with plastic bolts. That's right. Plastic bolts. To an untrained eye, they looked just like the kind you'd see in a DIY shop. The transparent bolt would have a nut that could be tightened. Don't ask me how it was supposed to work. I tried to get my head around it but in the end I decided against getting my corneas replaced by that particular guy.

Instead I found another specialist operating out of New Jersey. His office was underneath a four-star hotel. He explained that he performed surgery in the office and his patients then recovered upstairs, with clinical support on room service.

I trusted this new doctor and liked the plan he outlined to give another transplant a better chance of success, but as I thought more about it I knew that realistically there was no way I could have eye surgery in the States. Though the room service would almost certainly be better than NHS hospital food, if anything went wrong, I could be in serious trouble. I would be unable to travel back to the UK. This whole mission had already cost thousands of pounds and so far nothing had been done. As I looked at the specialist's charges – the first thing his receptionist wanted to know when I turned up for my initial appointment was 'cash or cheque' – I truly understood the value of the NHS. But they could no longer treat me and I was desperate to hang on to my sight in any way I could. I couldn't afford the private treatment, but neither could I afford to give up.

I wouldn't give up. I took the plunge and re-mortgaged my home.

Once the money was in place, one of the specialist's colleagues agreed to fly to the UK to assist with my transplant so that I was in no danger of being stranded in the States with time ticking on my tourist visa and escalating medical bills. He came to London a couple of weeks later and supported the team doing my eighth corneal transplant at a clinic on Harley Street, finishing it off with a thin layer of amniotic membrane that acted like cling film to hold the whole thing together. Amniotic membrane is the innermost layer of the protective sac surrounding an embryo. This was his signature move and a step I hadn't been through before. The American team had found that the membrane barrier helped to stop rejection in many previous patients as it acted as a natural healing plaster. I could only pray it worked for me too.

When I was sure I had perfect vision in the first eye treated, we went ahead and did the other. The second operation, which took place two months later using the same method, was another success. The crisis of impending blindness had been averted. I was skint but I could see again. That was worth everything to me.

Perhaps if I hadn't been a doctor myself, I would have taken 'no' for an answer when the UK specialists told me they'd done all they could after transplant number seven. It certainly would have been less expensive, but the pioneering transplant by the American specialist did restore my vision to 20:20. After a while, I didn't even need to use eye drops any more. I could go back to the job I loved and felt I could contribute again. I had my life back. Those last two transplants were worth every penny. Especially as they meant that I was able to rest my eyes upon, and fall in love with, the woman of my dreams.

3

Meeting Miss Right

My job in A&E was a fantastic challenge, but it was not so good for my social life. I loved what I did for a living. I loved meeting people from all walks of life and making a difference when they needed it most. But occasionally it would have been nice just to be able to make a plan to go out with my mates and actually stick to it. Instead, dinners with my friends and colleagues were often arranged at the very last minute and always had to be near the hospital to allow for the fact that I might be called back at any time. As a junior doctor in a short-staffed department that could be overwhelmed at any moment, I was permanently on call.

On one of those rare occasions when I did manage to meet friends as planned, we went to the champagne bar at St Pancras station – a swanky affair that runs the entire length of the Eurostar platform.

As I was scanning the huge bar for my mates, I noticed a woman sitting alone at a table, working on her laptop. I was instantly taken by her style. She was beautiful, composed and elegant as she tapped away at the keyboard. I would have loved to talk to her but I was there to meet my friends and she was obviously there to work. I didn't think there was any chance I would get to know her. Besides, I wasn't looking for love or even a flirtation right then. My career was still my main focus, especially since I'd had to take so much time out for my corneal transplants.

Of course, fate had other ideas.

Seema had been at a conference that day. As I walked into the bar, she caught me looking at her and assumed, since I was looking at her with such interest and smiled at her in such a confident and open way, that she must have met me somewhere before. Perhaps I was another conference delegate? Had she talked to me earlier that day? While one of my friends was in the gents' and the other one was taking a phone call, Seema seized the moment to reintroduce herself – at least, she thought she was reintroducing herself. I admitted to her at once that we hadn't previously met, but I was very glad to have a chance to make her acquaintance for the first time.

It was a brief opportunity. Seema was on her way back to Brussels, where she worked as a consultant in European public affairs. She told me that she'd grown up in Preston and gone to university in the Midlands before finishing her studies in Belgium. She'd also studied in Bordeaux. In the short time we had to get to know each other that evening, I grew more and more impressed and intrigued. She was feisty, strong and independent – so different to all the other girls I knew. I felt an instant connection. I could have spoken to her all night were it not for the announcement saying that her train to Brussels was ready for boarding.

Great, I thought as I waved her off. *That's just my luck. I've met an interesting, intelligent and stunningly beautiful woman and she lives in Belgium . . .* My friends teased me rotten as I re-joined them and told them all about it.

Seema and I had swapped numbers and both said we would love to meet up again, but I knew it was going to be difficult. We lived in different countries and we both had hectic, all-consuming careers. However, over the following months we kept in touch. We spoke on the phone as much as possible – often for hours at a time – and sent emails. The more I got to know Seema, the more I was convinced that even though the logistics weren't on our side, we had serious potential. I was determined not to let go of her. Finally, after a few missed connections, we managed our first proper date.

Seema was over in London again for work. We met up outside Bond Street Tube station and walked down to Mews of Mayfair, a quiet, unassuming bar. When at last we were face to face once more, Seema was every bit as interesting as I remembered and twice as beautiful. Though she's since admitted to me that she was nervous – which might be why she didn't let me get a word in edgeways – the connection between us now that we were across a table again was electric and intense. I was absolutely smitten.

After that, Seema and I spoke every single day and snatched every moment we could to be together. And sometimes it really was just a moment. After a meeting in London, Seema would text to say she had half an hour before she needed to catch her train back to Brussels. If I could get away, I would literally run from my office at the hospital to the Eurostar terminal at St Pancras to grab a coffee with her before she had to leave again.

After a year of such snatched moments of bliss – with us trying and failing to be in the same city at the same time on many a weekend – Seema got a new job, still doing what she loved in European affairs but finally based in London. Now that she was back in the UK, we were able to spend more time together and finally start to plan the future we'd both subconsciously known we wanted from the first time we met.

In many ways, we were chalk and cheese – we still are. I'm impulsive, energetic, easily bored and super-active. Seema is a planner, a thinker and a reader. Although she has a feisty side, she's generally calm and diplomatic compared to me. But we both knew that what we had was special. It was real love, of the kind that could go the distance. Very soon, it felt as though Seema had always been a part of my life, and I could no longer imagine being without her. Whenever I had any news to share – good or bad – it was Seema I wanted to talk to first. There was no one I would rather spend time with. No one else made me feel so happy or so understood. I knew that kind of connection was rare and precious indeed. Thankfully, she felt the same way.

After almost three years together, we decided it was time to get married. There was no real proposal as such. We'd just started talking about our future together as though marriage was a done deal. Once Seema and I had made the decision, we had to tell our parents. I remember telling mine. For various reasons, I ended up breaking the news to Dad in the car on a trip to MFI. My parents were delighted at the thought of having Seema as a daughter-in-law. They could see just how happy she made me and how much we loved one another.

Shortly afterwards, they met Seema's parents for the first time at a restaurant in Harrow. Part way through the meal, Dad disappeared. He was gone for so long that I started to worry. His going AWOL couldn't be creating a good impression with my future in-laws. When I went outside to look for him, I found him talking to James May, one of the presenters of *Top Gear*. Seema's dad was very impressed. Like my dad, he found the *Top Gear* gossip much more interesting than the wedding talk, which Mum and Seema's mother were already deeply into.

The Indian tradition is that there is a ceremony for every life event and our engagement was no exception. In my community it's the responsibility of the groom's family to arrange the engagement party, so I rented out the village hall at Send in Surrey for a Hindu blessing in front of three hundred friends and relations. Seema and I coordinated elaborate Indian outfits for the occasion and had a priest from our local temple to officiate. Then I got down on one knee and put a ring on Seema's finger. Once the formalities were done, of course we had a great big party.

Our engagement lasted just under a year and we had a civil marriage ceremony in March 2012 at Marylebone Town Hall. It was a relatively small affair followed by a reception and then drinks with a larger group of friends in the evening. In our minds the Marylebone marriage was a formality and an excuse to have a bit of a party. What we considered our real wedding – our big fat Indian wedding – took place two months later in Cheshire, not far from where Seema grew up.

We had more than 600 guests for this, our proper celebration. Friends and family members flew in from all over the world, coming from as far away as India, the United States and Canada. We booked out entire local hotels to accommodate and cater for them all over several days of events and rituals.

The party began on the Thursday evening. Over the next

couple of days, various family groups hosted different functions. Earlier in the year, Seema and her family had flown to India to get their outfits made. We each had ten changes of clothes for all the parties. The marriage ceremony itself was on the Sunday, at a beautiful Tudor house and grounds near Seema's home town. It was as though Bollywood had come to Cheshire.

We embraced every part of the traditional Hindu wedding ceremony, which is performed in the ancient language of Sanskrit by a Brahmin priest. The many rituals are taken from Hinduism's holy scriptures, the Vedas. They're performed under a beautiful, highly decorated canopy, called a Mandap, which also forms the altar. The Mandap represents the earth and its four directions, while its four pillars represent the parents of the bride and groom and their roles in raising them. In front of the Mandap is a sacred fire.

The fire is an important part of the ceremony. In a ritual known as Mangal Fera (Circling the Sacred Fire), Seema and I walked around the fire four times. The circles we made represented our vows to each other in Dharma (religion), Artha (wealth), Karma (love and family) and Moksha (spirituality). At the end of the last turn around the fire, there is a little game – whoever sits down first will run the house. Needless to say, on our wedding day Seema sat down first, though I won the other games later!

After the Mangal Fera, we took our vows in the form of Saptapadi, or 'Seven Steps', together. I led Seema as we recited the following mantras: 'We shall cherish one another in sickness and health, happiness and sorrow. We shall respect and take care of our family members. We shall share and support one another's ideas and ideals. We shall nourish one another's strengths, powers and good fortune. We shall be lifelong friends. We shall try to make our marital life richer day by day.' And finally, 'We shall sail through the seasons in spiritual unity.'

Until this point, Seema had been sitting on my right-hand side. Now we exchanged seats, so that Seema was on my left, representing her closeness to my heart. Next I offered Seema a black and gold beaded necklace, known as the mangalsutra, and red powder, called sindoor, for the centre parting of her hair – the traditional marks of a married woman.

Then we were bound together with a white cloth. One end was tied to Seema's veil and the other to my scarf. The tying of the cloth symbolized the union of our two souls.

Finally, a sacred thread, called a varmala was placed around us to protect us from evil. The varmala is a delicate thread which could easily break, to remind us that we needed to become one in behaviour, thought and body, to keep the varmala – and our marriage – intact. It was an emotional moment for both of us.

The wedding was amazing – loud, colourful and full of laughter. The soundtrack to the celebrations was a playlist that Seema and I had built up during the early days of our courtship, when we were living in different countries and I used to send her a 'song of the day' every morning. It was a wonderful privilege to be able to share our happiness with everyone we loved. And more than that, it was the most fantastic feeling in the world to be marrying my soulmate and best friend.

Seema and I didn't plan a honeymoon for right after the

wedding because, since people had come from so far to help us celebrate, it only felt right that we stuck around to spend some time with them. We arranged for some of them to come with us when we had our marriage blessed at a Hindu temple near Wolverhampton, which was en route from the wedding venue to my family home in Guildford.

It is Indian tradition to have the wedding in the bride's home town. The groom and his family have to come to fetch her, then take her back with them at the end of the celebrations. The bride is welcomed into her new home as the embodiment of the goddess Laxmi, the bringer of good fortune. As per that tradition, we wanted to make the journey from Cheshire to Guildford on the day of the actual ceremony. Since timings wouldn't permit us to visit a temple near the wedding venue or our new marital home in Guildford, midway it had to be.

We made it to the Wolverhampton temple with moments to spare. In our rush to get out of the car, Seema got out of one door and I got out of the other, forgetting that we were still tied together by our wedding outfits. Who was going to give in and follow the other one out of their door? Was that going to set the tone for the rest of our marriage? We got out of the same door in the end – my door – but, as Seema still reminds me to this day, only because I was on the pavement side.

The blessing ran late and we were caught up in traffic on the rest of the journey south. Though Seema and I weren't going to have an official honeymoon, we'd booked one night in the finest suite at a fancy hotel in Guildford. We were tired but happy when we arrived and took the keys to the posh room we had been looking forward to seeing.

I opened the door and pushed it aside so that Seema could walk in first. She switched on the light and suddenly screamed. Somebody was already in the big double bed in our honeymoon suite. On the bedside table were the chocolates and champagne our friends had ordered for us, both half finished. When the commotion of our arrival woke our Goldilocks up, he screamed too.

Goldilocks was embarrassed, but it wasn't his fault. The mix-up was entirely the hotel's mistake. All the same, there was nothing much they could do about it but apologize and book us into a smaller, ordinary double room for the night, with no chocs or fizz. By then we were too exhausted to complain. We were just so pleased to be properly married at last.

Seema and I soon settled into married life. We lived in Guildford, in the house I'd bought when I started working, and both commuted into London. I was still working in an A&E department in London, but now that I had Seema to consider and the possibility of a family in the future, I looked into retraining as a GP so I could work more locally. Cutting our commutes by moving back to London didn't seem like the solution we wanted. We loved our house in Guildford. It felt like a forever home. It was in a lovely neighbourhood, not far from Mum and Dad's. Since I'd enjoyed my childhood there so much, it seemed like a great place to consider raising our future children too. There were enough bedrooms for the family we longed for and a huge garden with lots of space to play.

About nine months after we married, Seema changed jobs,

moving to a new company and a more demanding role in the financial services sector, which took her to the United States from time to time. It was a step up – more pay, more responsibility and a new challenge, which she was hungry for. I was working the usual long, long days. Whenever we did manage a few days away, we made the most of it. We just wanted to be able to spend more time together.

Once we booked a weekend in Padstow, the pretty Cornish fishing village, but just before we were due to leave, my car had to go into the garage. The only hire car they could lend us was a convertible. Perfect for a road trip to Cornwall – though perhaps not a *winter* road trip! Regardless, we drove all the way there with the top down. I loved it. Fortunately, Seema was every bit as excited by speed and adventure as I was.

When we got to Padstow, Seema surprised me with a day at Rick Stein's cookery school. I had an amazing time. I've always enjoyed cooking – I still do – and it was brilliant to have the chance to learn new skills from the master. That weekend we were able to do the three things that we enjoyed the most – eating, drinking and talking. We explored the coast, hunting for the best fresh fish, the nicest wine, and the prettiest beaches. Cornwall was our happy place. It's a weekend I'll treasure for the rest of my life.

Of course, not all of our adventures were so picturesque. When we were driving home from visiting Seema's parents in Preston one weekend, we came upon a road traffic accident on the M1, involving a mini-bus and three cars. It looked serious. People were standing on the hard shoulder in a confused daze. I knew at once that we had to do what we could to help.

Because I was an official emergency responder, I had all my kit in the car. I put on my flashing lights, pulled over onto the hard shoulder and called the accident in. The air ambulance was already on its way.

The first people I attended to were a mum and her two children. They were OK but in shock. The weather had taken a turn and it was raining and cold. Since the road had been closed down and they couldn't get back to their own car, we decided it would be safer for them to sit in the back of our car with Seema to stay dry and warm while they waited. Meanwhile, a man in his eighties, who had been in one of the other vehicles, was trying to get back to his car by walking along the central reservation. He'd left his mobile phone there and wanted to contact his family. It took several of us to keep him from running out into the road and putting himself in danger.

I started checking people over as I waited for backup to arrive.

Eventually, once the emergency services were in attendance and we'd made sure everyone was safe, it was time for Seema and me to go on our way. As I got into the car, Seema warned me, 'Don't look back.'

'Why not?' I asked.

I'd seen for myself that all the people involved in the accident were safe. Thank goodness there had been no serious casualties. But now Seema's words started to worry me.

'Just don't look back,' she said again. 'Please, Amit.'

Of course, if you tell someone not to look back, that's the first thing they're going to do, right? And I did.

'Oh no!'

If I'd needed a sign that my wife knew me too well, this was it.

It turned out Seema wasn't worried that I would see something horrific on the road. She was worried that I would see the state of the back seats of my own car. The children who had been sitting in there to stay out of the rain had been eating crisps as they waited and wiping their muddy feet on my upholstery! There were crisp crumbs and dried mud all over the place.

'I told you not to look!' Seema sighed.

It was too late. Seema knew I wouldn't be able to drive all the way back to Guildford with my precious car in such a mess. I insisted that we stopped at the next service station and got out my portable vacuum.

Seema didn't complain about the detour. She just shook her head and laughed. She understood it was just the way I was. She knew me so well and tolerated so many of my quirks. I'd found my soulmate and we made a great team. Together, we were unconquerable. We were having a ball and we had such brilliant plans for the future. We had no idea what was just around the corner.

4

Lights Out

I'd had my last transplant – the one by the American specialist – prior to meeting Seema. She'd never been with me when I was going through a transplant rejection so she didn't know the signs. However, Seema could tell at once when I was tired, pointing it out long before it ever showed in my eyes and face. I would start to rub my head and gently pull at my hair. She'd noticed I had been doing that more and more often of late.

The day it happened was a Wednesday in November 2013. I'd gone to bed feeling tired and a little headachy, but no more than I usually did after a long day at work. After all, I didn't have the sort of job where I could turn up and faff about pretending to answer emails all day; it was full-on from the moment I arrived until the moment I managed to drag myself away.

I remember waking up that morning to the feeling of the sun on my face, expecting my busy daily routine to start all over again. Though it was winter, the warmth of the sunlight promised a lovely day. I turned off the alarm and sat up. As I blinked my eyes open, they felt a little gritty, but that wasn't so unusual. Likewise, my vision was hazy, but I didn't worry too much about it at first. I went to the bathroom and washed my face, expecting my vision to start to improve as I woke up properly. That was what usually happened. But this time, it didn't. Still, I didn't worry too much. Then, as I came out of the bathroom, Seema said, with her voice full of loving concern, 'Amit, I've found blood on your pillow.'

She and I both knew at once that it must have come from my eyes.

I was confused. What was going on that morning didn't match my previous experiences of corneal transplant rejection. It felt completely different. All the same, Seema and I agreed that there was no way I was going to work. Instead we went to the eye clinic at the Royal Surrey as soon as it was open at nine. Seema took the day off to come with me.

When Seema and I sat down to an anxious breakfast my sight was still blurred. It was like I was looking through dirty glass or at mist through a frosted bathroom window and with the passing minutes it wasn't getting any better. By nine o'clock, as we checked into the clinic, I knew that something serious was going on.

By ten o'clock, it was as though blinds were being pulled down on the edges of my sight. Darkness crept up from the bottom and down from the top of my field of vision. I tried to stay calm but when the consultant shone a light in my eyes to examine them, I felt a sharp pain unlike anything I'd experienced before. It took all I had not to scream.

The consultant told me that my corneas looked hazy, as though they'd been scratched. Yet at the same time he agreed with me that there were no obvious symptoms of rejection. At a loss as to what exactly was causing the changes in my vision and the pain that accompanied them, the consultant instructed that my eyes be bandaged overnight and I come back for a further examination the following day. Then I was discharged to go home with Seema and my parents, who had come to meet us at the hospital.

Mum and Dad were used to helping me get around after corneal transplants, but this was the first time I'd come home with both eyes bandaged at the same time. Seema helped me from the car into our house and guided me to an armchair in the living room. I sat there, helpless and afraid, while she and my parents did their best to make me comfortable. They spoke in hushed, worried tones, asking each other if there was something they should be doing. Was there anyone they should be calling? Anything more that could be done at the hospital?

I didn't speak much at all. I had too much to think about. In my head I was frantically running through possible scenarios as to what might happen next. My doctor's brain searched for likely diagnoses. There had to be a simple reason why my sight was failing. I even asked Seema to get my passport ready, in case the solution could be found overseas again. At the same time, I knew rationally that there was no way I would be able to fly with the pressure that was building inside my eyes. I couldn't deny it now. I could feel it. The deterioration had happened so suddenly.

I went to bed early, with my eyes still bandaged, mentally exhausted after a terrible day. Climbing under the covers beside me, Seema held me and reassured me that the next morning would bring better news. She was trying so hard to be positive. Of course the consultant would work out what was happening, she told me. I could only hope she was right.

I didn't sleep much. Overnight, the pain really kicked in. No amount of ibuprofen or paracetamol seemed to touch it. When I took the pads and bandages off my eyes the next morning, Seema confirmed that they were covered in mucus and traces of blood. It was hard to open my eyelids. Even the air hurt now. It was as though my eyeballs were two open wounds. Since I couldn't see anything when I looked in the mirror, Seema described my eyes for me. They were bright red and puffy, she said. My pupils had lost their shape and become strangely elongated, like the pupils in a cat's eyes. It was as though they had no structure to them any more. There was bruising all around my eyes too.

And I still couldn't see properly. Now it was like looking through milk.

At the hospital the consultant examined me again, but this time he was completely unable to see what was going on at the back of my eyes. The examination light stung too much. More drops were prescribed but the consultant could find no real answer as to why I was suddenly experiencing sight loss and likewise could think of no way to restore it. By the end of the appointment I could see only diffuse light and I couldn't keep my eyes open without extreme effort.

After that frustrating examination, I left the hospital with pads over my eyes held in place by sunglasses. I was advised to leave my eyes open if I could but to protect them with a shield. Back home, as Seema settled me in a chair again, my parents prepared the house as they used to do when I'd just had a transplant. Dad closed all the curtains to keep the house as dark as possible because the light burned my eyes and caused an unbearable migraine.

Later that day, we all sat down in the living room and tried to have a sensible conversation about what was going on and what my options were. Surely I wasn't really going blind? After all I'd done to preserve my sight, it simply wasn't possible. There had to be a solution. I could hear the worry in my loved ones' voices as they agreed with me.

'We'll find a way through this, Amit,' said Dad. 'There's got to be a cure.'

'Of course there has,' said Mum.

But the reality was that all of us were in denial.

Over the space of thirty-six hours, my life changed forever. The only way I can describe losing my sight is that it was like sinking to the bottom of a very deep pool. At first you can see the ripples, but then it gets darker, darker and darker, and you can feel the light just fading away. Your body feels numb and it goes quiet and suddenly you're in a different world.

Over the next few days I shut down and barely spoke to anyone. Not even Seema. I responded to her kind and careful inquiries with brusque single word answers. The pain in my eyes was unbearable and I'd been put on an extremely high dose of painkillers that left me dopey and out of it. At the same time, I couldn't sleep. I was in my own little world. Our family GP, who had known me since I was five years old, came to see me. She prescribed sleeping tablets but they made me giddy and unstable and left me feeling worse than ever.

Now that I couldn't see anything but diffuse light, I was fast losing track of time. I didn't know whether it was the middle of the day or the middle of the night. It all looked the same to me. As a result, my body didn't really know when to go to bed or when to eat. You have no idea how much of your daily routine is governed by natural light until you can no longer see it. It was frightening how quickly my physiological rhythms became unmoored from the clock.

Fortunately, Seema's employers were understanding and allowed her to take compassionate leave so that she could be with me twenty-four seven in those terrible early days. Mum and Dad also dropped everything to be there and do what they could to support us. They had retired and sold their shop shortly before Seema and I married. We were all grateful that they had the time to help.

A couple of weeks passed. That period of time is hard for me to remember very clearly. The meds I was taking made me so spaced out, yet I was still experiencing tremendous pain. I couldn't keep my eyes open. I was given a special visor to wear – a flexible wraparound plastic mask that kept the light from coming in at the edges. I went to the clinic again and again. At some point my case was referred to the specialists at the famous Moorfields Eye Hospital in London and soon the diary was packed with dozens of visits to the clinic there.

At every appointment, a never-ending train of doctors and medical students came to examine me. With each new person who entered the room, I felt a cruel flicker of hope. Maybe this stranger would be the one who could solve the mystery of what was happening. Maybe they would have seen a case like mine before and have a simple solution. But nobody had any useful answers.

As Christmas approached, we were no closer to knowing exactly what had happened to my eyes than on that first day. After a while, I told Seema and my parents that I didn't want to go to Moorfields any more. I was starting to feel like a guinea pig and I no longer had any faith that submitting myself to endless examinations would help.

Looking back, I think I knew that first Wednesday morning in November that my sight was gone forever. But it was almost a month later that I finally accepted I was blind.

Seema took me to Moorfields for what would be my last appointment there. For the first time, I asked her to sit in the waiting room while I saw the consultant alone. Seema had been right beside me for everything, but that day I worried that her presence in the consulting room would inhibit me from saying what I needed to say, which was that I wanted to be certified blind and be signed off from any more painful and needless investigations. I had to take this awful step on my own.

The consultant knew I had not given up on my sight easily, but he also saw that to move forward I had to let it go. Quickly and professionally he did the necessary assessment and told me that I would be certified as severely sight impaired (blind). Once the certificate was signed, he explained, I would be discharged from his care into that of my local authority. The rest would be in their hands. I assured him that I understood and asked him to go ahead, though we still didn't know what had caused this sudden loss of sight to happen. Once the deed was done, I thanked the consultant and his team for all their efforts and then asked Seema to take me home.

Only later would we discover that blood vessels in my eyes had burst. Our bodies are full of these tiny vessels, which supply blood to our organs, and those that supply our eyes can be damaged just like any others. Even something as simple as a knock to the eye could cause some injury.

I've never suffered from high blood pressure, which can increase your risk of blood vessel damage, and there were never any signs that warned me I was having problems. Because I'd had corneal transplants, I had my eyes checked every three months. But throughout the various conversations, medical consultations and assessments afterwards, the one thing the doctors agreed on was that I had experienced a pressure build-up in the vessels that supply blood to my retinas, which then led to bleeding in the eyes. This was followed instantly by the hazy vision I'd had in the morning. That's what resulted in my loss of vision. There was no big bang diagnosis, no clear reason as to why it happened, and even now the cause is still a mystery. But what it has resulted in, alongside the already life-changing sight loss, is constant pain. The lack of blood flow to my eyes resulted in a lot of nerve damage, and this still causes me agony every day.

Being certified blind was a heartbreaking moment. I wanted to cry but I waited until we were home and locked myself away in the bathroom so that Seema wouldn't see me break down. As broken-hearted as I was, I knew that Seema was devastated too. She had been through so much with me and remained so strong and so hopeful. She needed comfort as much as I did, but, right then, I had to be alone to take it all in. I couldn't bear her sadness as well as mine. I just wasn't tough enough.

Alone in the bathroom, I gave into my grief and howled for everything I had lost. My worst nightmare had come true at last, after all those years I'd spent battling to hang on to my vision, with all those uncomfortable lenses, all those failed corneas, after my crazy trip to the States and that last pair of pioneering transplants. Despite all that hope and all that effort, I had to accept that I would never see again.

5

A Cry for Help

I'd like to say that the worst was over, but now that I was registered blind, things got really tough.

My eyes weren't just useless, they also hurt like hell. Twenty-four hours a day, I felt as though someone was sticking needles in my eyeballs and twisting them for good measure. When my eyes weren't shut, they stung like they'd been rubbed with extra-rough sand paper. I desperately needed powerful pain relief, but the opiates I'd been given were messing up my body. I couldn't cope without them and yet in many ways they were making things much worse.

I'd been such an active person, but now I spent my days sitting in a chair. I was sliding into depression. I could think only of the negatives and hear nothing but pity in the voices of the people who spoke to me. Though Seema and my parents did their best to be positive whenever they talked to me, the pessimistic voice in my head was far louder than any kind words they might have to say. And there were moments when Seema and Mum and Dad really didn't know what to say. They wanted to comfort me and keep me going, but at the same time they didn't want to demean my experience. No matter how hard they tried to strike the right balance between hope and understanding, I was quick to take things badly. I'd always been a laid-back kind of person but now the littlest thing could make me angry. Everyone around me was walking on eggshells.

All day long the voice in my head kept up a running commentary of doom. Dr Amit Patel, the adventurous young A&E specialist, was gone forever. Everything was slipping away from me. I'd been signed off from the job I loved in a single excruciating phone call with my boss that left me on the verge of tears. I was the disabled guy in the corner now. I had no career and no purpose. I was a useless waste of space. Everyone pitied me. Seema would leave me. That's what people were saying, I was sure. Why wouldn't she? The man she'd fallen in love with no longer existed. He'd been replaced by an overgrown child who couldn't even cut up his food without assistance. Seema was young and beautiful, intelligent, funny and kind. She could have had anyone. She certainly deserved better than a blind man. No matter how hard Seema tried to reassure me that she was going nowhere, I wouldn't hear it. My life as I'd known it was over and I had no future. Seema didn't have to be dragged down too.

As I sat in that chair, wearing my pyjamas and letting the days pass by, I was deep in mourning for the loss of the person I once was. It wasn't only my sight that had been taken from me but my confidence, my independence, my drive and my passion for life. I'd been a strong man who faced every challenge with a smile. Now I was a scared child, afraid of my own shadow (if only I could have seen it).

One night at the end of December 2013, I hit a new low. I'd been certified blind. I wasn't sleeping because of the pain in my eyes but I hated taking my pain meds. It was like I couldn't even walk straight when I was on them. Whenever I stood up, my legs felt like jelly and I didn't trust that I wouldn't fall over. However, without the medication, my head was on fire. Even the central heating hurt, as it dried my eyes out. I couldn't seem to control my body temperature. One minute I was in a T-shirt and shorts. Next, I was swaddled in a blanket. All I could do was sit with my head against the wall, which at least was cool and soothing. I felt like an animal, trapped in a cage of despair.

The negative voice in my head was having a field day that evening, comparing where I'd been the previous year with where I was now and where I was likely to be in another year's time. 'It's only going to get worse,' the voice told me with absolute certainty. 'And Seema will definitely have given up on you by then.'

I wasn't thinking straight. I just wanted to sleep. I just wanted to silence that negative voice for a minute or two. I had no real concept of time, of whether it was day or night. I was so tired and in so much pain. I would do anything just to get some rest. Unwittingly, I took a whole week's worth of sleeping tablets in a day.

When I realized what I'd done, I told Seema immediately and she called our GP, who insisted that I was taken straight to hospital. The effects of my various medications alongside the sleeping tablets meant that I was barely able to register where I was, let alone what was happening around me. Thank goodness I avoided having my stomach pumped – the doctor who saw me said I'd just have to wait until the drugs cleared my system – but I knew from my many years in A&E that under the circumstances I wouldn't be allowed home without a psychiatric evaluation.

I had that evaluation. It was a turning point.

During my time as a doctor, I'd treated many people who'd taken overdoses and had often heard the term 'a cry for help' used to describe their desperate actions. At last I truly understood what that really meant. With that dose of sleeping tablets, I had unknowingly sent up my own cry for help and thank goodness it had been heard.

I was quickly referred to a counsellor, called Jenny, who had experience of visual impairment, having grown up with a blind parent. When I explained to her that I wasn't trying to take my own life but just wanted to feel normal again, she understood at once what I meant. She knew that I didn't need to be kept in hospital, rather that I needed more support so I could be happier at home. Since I lost my sight, Seema and I had been coping with no real help from anyone but our immediate families. We needed more support. I especially needed to find a way to manage my pain so that it didn't leave me feeling so out of it the whole time.

With the help of Jenny and our GP, I straight away began to reduce the dosage of painkillers and changed some of the other medication that I was still having to take. It made an immediate difference. As some of the drugs left my system, my thinking began to clear. I started to be able to sense what time of day it was again. It turned out that it hadn't just been about not being able to see. Likewise my appetite came back, and being able to get a few solid hours of sleep on the odd occasion made all the difference.

The one thing that remained was the constant pain in my

eyes. No amount of drugs would help to relieve that so I needed to find my own coping mechanism. Keeping my mind busy helped during the day, but the nights were very tough – I was never able to dampen the pain in order to sleep, but I found that having background noise helped to distract me a bit. I listened to LBC all night long with headphones in my ears. Even to this day, it's the only thing that helps me to sleep at night.

After my impromptu hospital visit, the local authority sent someone round to assess my situation fairly quickly. They had received the notification from my consultant that I had been registered blind and I was now officially under their care. My visitor was visually impaired himself, in his sixties or seventies. He came to tell me what I should expect from life as a visually impaired person and what I could do to make the best of it.

'It's not all bad,' he said.

I wasn't doomed to a life of helplessness and dependency, he promised me. My overly negative idea of what the rest of my life held for me was all wrong. He talked about his own sight loss journey and about learning to use a white cane and to read braille. There were all sorts of new technologies to help me navigate the world too. He advised me to embrace assistive technology for a start. He helped to ease some of my anxieties just through the sheer fact of being present and talking me through things.

'You're a young man,' said my new friend as we wrapped up our meeting. 'You can still make something of your life if you want to. The only limits are your own expectations.'

Then I had a small stroke of luck. The local authority

worker told me about a trial which a local charity called Sight for Surrey was running with Royal Holloway University. They were going to give twenty-five visually impaired people counselling over the phone while a further twenty-five would get counselling in person. I was lucky enough to be chosen for the second group – those who would get to be in the same room as their counsellor – and was signed up for twice weekly sessions for the next two months.

It made all the difference. Though, of course, Seema and my parents were always there for me whenever I needed to talk, I hadn't been able to open up to them. I know that was hard for Seema in particular. She felt shut out and frustrated that she couldn't help me process what was going on. Perhaps I had been foolishly trying to protect her from the worst of it. At the same time, rather than face their pity, I hadn't even told many of my friends what had happened so they weren't able to offer any support either.

Being able to speak to a therapist who wasn't personally invested in my life allowed me to explore my darkest feelings without worrying that I would be upsetting anyone. I was angry, frustrated and lost. It was so unfair and I just couldn't understand why this had happened to me. On top of it all, I felt useless and helpless. Getting those angry thoughts out was cathartic. Ironically, it was also easier to believe the good news – that things could and would get better – because it was coming from someone impartial who had no interest in sugar-coating their words.

Like the visually impaired chap who'd visited me at home, the therapist did her best to convince me that I was not destined to spend the rest of my life sitting in an armchair until someone else deigned to take me out. Plenty of visually impaired people live very active lives, she assured me. It was up to me to make the effort to regain my independence. She encouraged me to start with white cane training.

As I heard about what the training would involve, the ghost of the old Amit – the crazy young man who had learned to ski and jumped out of an aeroplane for fun – woke up and decided here was a challenge worth exploring. I said I'd do it.

The therapist quickly arranged for me to have my first cane. It was a 'symbol cane', which is a short white stick that you hold in front of your body in the way a soldier holds a ceremonial sword. It looks like a wand and lets people around you know that you're visually impaired.

I prayed that wand would turn out to be magical for me, but the fact was it wouldn't enable me to go out on my own, which was what I really wanted. It was too short to help me work out if there were obstacles on the path ahead so it wasn't the aid to independence I longed for. It felt useless. All it really did was warn people to get out of my way because I couldn't see them coming – assuming they even understood that the symbol cane meant I was visually impaired and not an overgrown Harry Potter fan.

Unfortunately, holding the symbol cane left me more despondent than ever. Having just about scrambled out of the abyss that led me to swallow those pills, I hit another low. The negative voice continued its commentary. I was sure I would never be able to go out alone again.

6

A Turning Point

When I got my symbol cane, we were still living in our house in Guildford. Seema had gone back to work and was commuting into London every weekday again. It wasn't an ideal situation.

With Seema at least an hour and a half away when she was at the office, my parents insisted they would put the plans they'd had for their retirement on hold to be with me whenever I needed them. Their help was invaluable. They were our safety net, not only practically but psychologically too. I don't think Seema would have been able to go back to work at all without knowing that Mum and Dad were on hand in case of an emergency. They lived just a few minutes away.

All the same, I didn't want to have to rely on my parents so heavily. I felt guilty and frustrated that they'd dropped everything for me. They should have been enjoying their hard-earned retirement, not worrying about their thirty-two-year-old son.

As the months wore on, I started to spend more time home alone to try to bring some normality back to my life, but my early efforts weren't always successful. I began to realize just how much I'd previously been able to do without really thinking about it. Take walking up and down the stairs. Now

I needed to count them out so that I didn't fall. I had to memorize how many steps there were from the living room to the kitchen or feel my way around by tracking the walls and sweeping my foot in front of me to find any obstacles.

Without sight, even the simplest things were now ridiculously complicated. One day while Seema was at work, I decided I would make myself a cup of tea. It seemed like it should be easy enough. To measure the level of the water I'd poured into the cup, I stuck my finger in, not really thinking about how hot the water would actually be. Of course, I burned my finger and in whipping my hand away, I sent the cup flying. It shattered on the kitchen floor. Still, I was determined I wasn't going to call Seema or Mum or Dad to tell them what had happened. Instead, I fumbled around the kitchen cupboards until I found the dustpan and brush. I got down on my knees and cleared up the broken crockery myself. I thought I'd done a reasonable job until Seema arrived home early.

She'd been calling me for an hour but I'd left my phone in the living room, hadn't been able to find it again and didn't know she'd been trying to get in touch. When she couldn't reach me, Seema panicked and came racing home to find out what was going on.

'What on earth happened?' she cried as soon she saw me.

I was covered in blood. While clearing up the pieces of the broken cup, I had badly cut my hands. Thanks to the pain-killing meds I was still taking, I didn't have a clue. My hands were numb and I hadn't felt a thing as the sharp edges of the broken china sliced deep into my skin. I was a danger to myself.

It was shortly after this incident that Seema decided something had to change. We loved our house in Guildford but her daily commute was becoming a problem. If the trains and Tubes were running well, Seema could be home in about an hour and a half. If they weren't – and they often weren't – then your guess was as good as mine. There were occasions when it took Seema more than twice as long as it should to get from her office to our house and she worried that in an emergency she couldn't be with me as quickly as she needed to be.

But what was the solution? Seema loved her job in Canary Wharf. She liked her colleagues and her boss, who had been incredibly supportive and understanding when she needed to take time off during the early days of my sight loss. Finding a position nearer to home that would give Seema the same job satisfaction with an employer who would also be accommodating of our circumstances was going to be difficult. But since there was no chance I would be going back to work any time soon, we needed Seema's income. Since that horrible day in November, Seema had become the sole breadwinner, the carer, the everything . . . The pressure on her to keep us both afloat was immense. It was not what she had signed up for when we married. I felt helpless as we did our best to come up with a workable solution.

In the end, it was Seema who pointed out the answer that had been staring us in the face all along. The company Seema worked for wasn't ever going to relocate, but we could . . .

'I think we should move to London,' she said.

'London? You're kidding.'

It seemed to me like the exact opposite of what would make our lives easier. London is hard enough to deal with at the best of times, but for someone who was newly blind, it would surely be a nightmare. Without sight, the thought of a walk down Guildford High Street – the chocolate-box cobbled street I had grown up around – was a world of terror for me. I was petrified of navigating the crowds even here. Walking through one of the busiest cities on earth would be like going into hell. All that traffic. All those people. I'd never be able to cope. In any case, for what we could hope to get for our lovely house in Guildford, we'd end up living in a shoebox in London. We wouldn't be able to afford a garden such as we had right then. Not that I was using the garden any more. All the same, I had plenty of reasons why we couldn't make the move.

Refusing to be put off, Seema continued to set out her case. Of course, she hadn't just come up with the idea off the top of her head. Seema being Seema, she'd weighed up all the pros and cons before even suggesting the idea to me. Yes, it would be expensive. Yes, we'd probably have to swap our proper house and garden for a flat the size of a shed, but at the same time, Seema could swap her sometimes difficult commute for a taxi ride if she needed to be with me at short notice. That would be a huge weight off her mind. While Guildford Borough Council had been very good in terms of giving me the care I needed so far, in London we would have access to much better services to help me move forward, plus much better public transport to get around too, when I was ready. Seema also agreed that though they would have done anything to make our lives easier, we couldn't always rely on my parents to be available at the click of my fingers.

She had already begun to research the various London boroughs to see which had the best record regarding support for the visually impaired. She'd settled on the borough of Newham. This east London area had benefitted enormously from the Olympics, which saw it receive a huge level of investment. It provided amazing services for residents with disabilities as well as being an easy commute into her office. In Newham, I could learn to use a white cane for real – one that was longer and would enable me to feel ahead of me for obstructions. I could forget the Harry Potter wand for good.

Though my first instinct was to think this was Seema's maddest idea yet, she gradually talked me into it. A move to London sounded frightening, but ironically it would offer us much more independence. Wasn't that what I wanted?

Within days we started to look for somewhere new to live. We decided on the Docklands area.

We quickly found the ideal flat in a fairly new block in a gated community by the docks and the river Thames. At the development's centre was a listed building converted into a bar/restaurant with a gym underneath. There was a convenience store on site too, so it wasn't isolated and we would have access to some amenities without needing to travel too far. Best of all, it was a short walk from a Docklands Light Railway station where Seema could catch a train that would whisk her to her office in Canary Wharf in just a few minutes. If the DLR wasn't working, it was close enough for her to walk home in an emergency. The flat was on the fifth floor but the building had a lift. Inside, the flat itself was well laid out and all on one level. There were no tricky stairs for me to navigate. What's more, the development had security staff who were on hand day and night. It would be perfect for our purposes. We booked a viewing.

Seema held my hand as we walked through the door of the building and made our way to the lift. Her audio description started from the very minute we walked in. She told me about the colour of the walls in the foyer, the artwork on display and the location of the postboxes. On reaching the flat I got a running commentary as we walked from room to room – the size of the windows, the style of bathroom fittings, the layout of the kitchen. I could hear the excitement in her voice as she took my hand and placed it on the kitchen tap, saying, 'You would have chosen this yourself,' (and she was right). Then she took me over to feel the chunky door handles, which she knew I would also love. Every inch of the flat was described to me in the most colourful detail, with emphasis on the features she knew I would like. We put in an offer immediately. We were on our way.

Two days later, we learned we'd been gazumped. We made a higher offer. We were gazumped again. It happened again and again until the price was completely out of our reach. In our minds, that flat had been ours and we were very disappointed not to get it. However, just a few weeks later, the estate agent called Seema to say another flat had come onto the market. Same building, same layout. But this one was on the first floor.

As soon as Seema called to say what had happened, I knew we had to act fast. She wanted me to visit the flat before we put an offer in. We could view it that day, she said. But, of course, she was in London and I was in Guildford.

The idea that this might be our dream flat galvanized me

and made me take a risk I hadn't dared to before. There was no way we were going to lose this one. I was going to London.

I nervously called for a taxi to take me to Guildford train station, explaining to the cab firm that I was blind and needed the driver to come to my door and guide me to the car. I waited by the front door, clutching my symbol cane for dear life, until I heard the doorbell ring. The softly spoken taxi driver offered me his elbow to guide me to his waiting car, not seeming the least bit phased at my situation. On the short journey to the station, all I could think of was whether I was trying to run before I could walk. Quite literally.

On arrival at the train station, I was taken aback by the noise and commotion around me, something that I wouldn't have even noticed a few months earlier. The taxi driver escorted me to a member of station staff and I asked them to put me on the right train for London Waterloo. The staff member explained that they would call ahead to Waterloo to say I'd need assistance there. They had processes in place, including letting station staff at the other end know which carriage I was sitting in, to ensure I would be met off the train. After the train, I'd also need help getting to the right Tube platform to take the Jubilee Line to the DLR, where Seema would be waiting so that we could do the last part of the journey together. It would be straightforward. I hoped.

It was the first time I'd been out of the house alone since I lost my sight three months earlier and now I was going to London! I didn't even have a proper white cane to guide me, just that symbol cane which I clutched like a talisman. It felt like a crazy undertaking and yet at the same time I was excited. It seemed as though fate was throwing me a line. It was exhausting and at some point it started raining, but when it all went well I was exhilarated. The taxi driver, the station staff and the staff at the Tube all worked in harmony to get me to where I needed to be. When Seema met me on the platform, I could tell by her voice that she was thrilled I had managed the whole journey without her or my parents. It was a good omen. She linked her arm through mine and we set off to see the flat that I was already sure would be our home.

I could hear in the way she spoke to the estate agent that Seema loved the flat. We walked round it together and she confirmed that it was exactly the same layout as the flat we'd just missed out on. She told me that the place was beautifully finished and would be easy for me to get about in. And because it was on the first floor, it had direct access to a large raised terrace which was perfect for a BBQ and having friends over. At this point, we didn't know how important that terrace would become.

After the viewing, Seema and I went to the nearby bar to discuss making an offer. By the time we'd finished our drinks, we both knew we wanted the flat to be ours. I'd gone from being alarmed at the idea of moving to London to agreeing with Seema that it was the perfect solution. I couldn't wait. I could already imagine us living there.

Just six weeks later, in May 2014, we moved into the new flat. We quickly got to know the security staff and the concierge, who did everything they could to help us settle in. While Seema was out at work, the security guys would often invite me into their office for a cuppa. I loved the new place from the start.

More importantly, I could tell that the move to London

had made Seema so much more relaxed. Knowing that there were people just a few steps away that I could call on for help twenty-four seven was – as Seema had suggested it would be – a huge weight off her mind. I could hear excitement in her voice again. The Seema I'd fallen in love with in the champagne bar at St Pancras station was back. Or at least a part of her was.

Everyone goes through their own journey when they lose their sight – depression, anger and frustration are only a part of the story. The impact on those around you shouldn't be underestimated. I was only really beginning to understand that, since that awful day in November, Seema had suffered just as much as I had. She needed support and reassurance as much as I did.

Seema's hunch that a move to London would be a good thing for us was absolutely right. After months of tiptoeing around each other, of not saying everything we really wanted to for fear of causing each other more pain, we started to feel closer again. I stopped fearing that she was going to leave me because I finally realized just how hard Seema would fight to keep us together. She would move heaven and earth. She would certainly move house. We were still the team we'd promised to be on our wedding day. Our love was as strong as ever.

Thanks to Seema's inspired decision to leave Guildford, it wasn't long before I too felt relaxed and confident enough to take the next step in my journey. In the autumn of 2014, just under a year since I lost my sight, I signed up for white cane training.

7

Learning to Walk Again

As Seema had discovered during her research, the London Borough of Newham had received a great deal of investment in 2012 and that included funding for their Community Resource Centre, where visually impaired people (VIPs) could get support and training in all aspects of independent living, from using a white cane to learning how to cook.

As soon as we moved into our new place, we went ahead with our plan to take advantage of that facility. It wasn't easy. It was a long while before anyone at the centre even returned our calls and our first scheduled face-to-face meeting was cancelled at the last minute after Seema had already taken the day off work to be there. It was frustrating to say the least. Thankfully Seema is a brilliant lobbyist who wouldn't take 'no' for an answer when it came to my needs. She kept on pushing and pushing until eventually I was given a date for an assessment.

The rehab worker who did that assessment was senior practitioner Pauline Acott. After a careful interview, in which she ascertained how sight loss had impacted my daily living – especially my mobility and communication – she agreed that I should try long cane training. She explained that the symbol cane I'd been given was really only practical for people with residual sight or just as a means for letting people know the situation when I was out with someone else. Lots of people hate the idea of using a long cane, but Pauline assured me it would open up a whole new world.

Pauline also recommended lessons in braille. Though there are lots of types of software that will read an email or a book to you these days, I still wanted to have a means of reading in the way I was used to – that is, to myself, privately. Braille was the only answer.

Deciding to learn braille gave me another incentive to wean myself off the heavy pain medication I was still taking: you can't read it with numb fingers. Slowly, I cut back on the tablets, trying to find the elusive balance between controlling the pain in my eyes and being able to feel with my fingertips again. I also began to rub sea salt onto my finger pads to help make them more sensitive.

To take my mind off the pain as I dropped the dose of my meds, I had started listening to music again, returning to the playlist I'd put together for our wedding from the 'songs of the day' I sent Seema when we were first dating. The songs ran the gamut from R&B classics to tunes from cheesy Bollywood movies.

When I lost my sight, it was as though the music stopped too. For a long time, I couldn't bear to listen to the tunes that represented such a happy time in my life. Now, however, I felt as though I could have music around me again. I was beginning to feel optimistic.

Things finally started to go my way. It had taken so long for me to get an initial assessment in Newham that I worried it would be months before my long cane and braille training started, but Pauline was able to get my programme in place relatively quickly. I was assigned to her colleague Stella Kamangirira.

As soon as Seema and I met Stella at the centre, I knew I liked her. Stella was extremely experienced in her field, having worked both as a teacher for visually impaired children and in the braille library at the University of Zimbabwe. Her calm, warm, no-nonsense manner helped me believe that I could achieve all my new objectives with her support – namely, becoming independent, more confident and getting some focus back into my life. She signed me up for two sessions a week for two months and assured me that she'd have me reading braille and getting around London with my new cane before I knew it.

I was excited at the prospect of getting out and about at last, but, motivated as I was to get going, it was still quite the shock to the system to begin my lessons for real. Learning to do anything new as an adult is hard and I was about to find out how difficult it was to learn to 'walk' again. Because walking with a white cane isn't as easy or instinctive as it may look.

For that reason, my first few sessions with Stella were at the centre in Newham, which has long corridors where I could make mistakes in safety. To begin with, I needed to find the right length of cane for me, based on my stride, speed of walking and position of my arms. This alone took a bit of trial and error. One thing no one tells you when you start using a cane is how much your arm aches from holding it out all day long!

The second key element to finding the white cane for me

was the tip of it – what kind did I need? Prior to meeting Stella, I had no idea there were different types. Now I learned that some canes have rolling balls on the end, called marshmallow tips, which allow you to roll it smoothly across a surface to feel for changes and obstacles. Other canes have solid ends and need to be tapped as you walk. I found that the marshmallow tip suited me best.

The third stage was learning the technique to stepping forward while swinging the cane safely, left, right, left, right, so that I could scan the area around me (i.e. 'read' what's ahead) without endangering everyone else in my vicinity. Definitely easier said than done.

And finally, I needed to learn *how* exactly I could move around safely. Swinging my cane as I walked in a straight line was one thing but how could I get from A to B when I needed to cross roads, go up and down steps or even take an escalator? This is where I uncovered a secret code to which most people are oblivious.

Have you ever noticed all those bumps on the pavement close to a pedestrian crossing? Or perhaps when you step off the train onto the platform? Or how about ridges like corduroy in the paving when you approach stairs at a station? They all mean something when you're visually impaired – the bumps are 'tactile', which means they're easily identified by a white cane. They indicate crossings, or dropped kerbs, depending on the layout. The vertical ridged tactile paving means you're approaching steps and horizontal ridges mean there is a bike lane. Where there is a longer tail of bumps on the approach to a pedestrian crossing, this is intended to guide a visually impaired person straight to the crossing button.

And then what? Have you ever pushed the button and waited for the green man to appear? Many crossings at busy junctions don't have audible notifications letting you know when it's safe to cross. Instead, a visually impaired person needs to place their hand under the button on the crossing box to feel for a little cone that spins when it's time to walk. I had no idea about any of these things until I started my white cane training.

Fortunately, Stella was on hand to teach me the secret language of the street in her calm and patient way. When she was confident that I had mastered getting around the corridors of the centre, she took me out onto the quiet streets nearby for some real-world practice. Later, she came to our home and helped me to work out some useful routes, identifying the tactiles and other landmarks – such as post boxes – that would help me find my way around my neighbourhood.

Stella also taught me that getting around with a long cane isn't just about sweeping my way from one landmark to the next. She reminded me that I could also use my sense of hearing to gain information about the environment. She helped me to properly tune in to the sound of approaching cars. Listening carefully would tell me how fast they were driving. The different sounds my cane made as I moved it across different surfaces would also help me work out where I was.

Stella's teaching didn't end with the practicalities. She also helped me understand how I needed to interact with the public. For example, how to be assertive and even how to turn down help when I didn't need it. She told me that some of her students complained that well-meaning members of the public would 'help' them to places they didn't want to be. I began to understand why Pauline had warned me back at my initial assessment that a visually impaired person needs to be psychologically as well as physically ready to step out with a white cane.

It was a lot to take in.

Getting to grips with being blind was soon keeping me as busy as a full-time job. Whenever I had a sniff of something that might give me more independence, I threw myself into it. The minute I swapped my symbol cane for a proper full-length cane, I practised walking alone around the complex where we lived in between official training sessions. The security guards would watch me on CCTV as I swept my way around the building and its gardens for hours on end.

'Gave us a scare, you did,' they told me after they watched me sweep my way up and down the building's stairwell. They also told me that whenever I was doing my white cane practice in the garden, I had an audience. Hearing the rolling sound of the cane on the path, neighbours would stop what they were doing and come out to watch me from their balconies. Knowing that so many people were ready to help if I got into trouble gave me another shot of confidence.

Because I was so determined to get my training done and therefore practised whenever I could, within a month Stella decided that I'd made enough progress to be allowed to use my cane to get from home to the training centre in Canning Town without her.

'You're ready,' she said.

It took me a couple more days to feel as ready as Stella

seemed to think I was, but eventually I managed to psych myself up enough to say I would give it a try. It was quite a complicated journey, involving a pelican crossing on the walk to the DLR station, three stops on the train and a bus ride, but I knew I had to go for it. It would be like taking the stabilizers off a bike. If I could get to the centre alone, I could go anywhere. All the same, I think I felt less nervous when I jumped out of a plane as a teenager.

On the designated morning, I accepted the good wishes of the security staff and tap-tapped my way out of the complex into the big wide world. I kept my head high as I walked to the DLR. A smile spread across my face as I successfully navigated the crossing without assistance and made the five-minute walk to the station without incident. I found the lift without help and got as far as the correct platform entirely under my own steam. It was there that things started to go less well.

Unlike the Tube, DLR trains don't have drivers. To complicate things further, DLR train doors don't open automatically, as the doors on the Tube do. You have to press a button to make them open. Needless to say, if you can't see the button, it's no easy task trying to find it before the train sets off again . . . It also doesn't help that DLR trains aren't all the same length, so there's no way to make an educated guess as to where the doors are. Fortunately, there are on-board guards who are supposed to look out for people who need assistance when boarding or alighting.

However, that day, my first day as a qualified white cane user, I could find no one on the platform to help me onto the train. I listened in frustration as one, two, then three trains passed without my being able to get onto any of them. The guards obviously didn't notice me. If there was anyone else on the platform, they didn't make themselves known and offer to help. Eventually, determined not to miss a fourth train, when the train pulled into the platform and I heard its doors open, I yelled out, 'Could somebody please help me get on?'

This time a train guard got out to come and find me. He helped me to climb on board but that was it. Unlike on previous occasions when I'd been with Seema or Stella, this guard didn't offer to find me a seat. I was too nervous to ask anyone else for help so I just stood by the door, doing my best to keep my balance as the train took off along the track.

A couple of stops later – I think it was at ExCel – I heard a lot of people get on. Maybe even as many as thirty or forty people, by the sound of things. The carriage was suddenly filled with noise and chatting and I could sense that there were other people standing close by me near the doors. The train took off again. There were so many conversations going on at once, it was hard for me to focus on any one voice in particular, but after a while, a single voice stood out above the others.

'Are you staring at me?' the man asked.

I didn't respond.

'Are you staring at me?' he demanded again. 'Stop staring at me.'

With a feeling of rising dread, I gradually realized that the angry speaker was directing his comments at me.

'Stop bloody staring!'

This time he shoved my shoulder and yelled right in my face. He was so close, I could feel his breath.

'I'm sorry,' I said at once. 'I didn't actually realize I was staring at you. I'm blind. I didn't even know I was looking in your direction. I'm sorry.'

My apology was not enough.

'I don't care if you are fucking blind,' he said and shoved me again. This time it was hard enough to unbalance me. My legs went one way. My long cane – of which I had recently been so proud – went flying in the opposite direction. I ended up on the floor.

The buzz of commuters talking immediately stopped; the train carriage was suddenly absolutely silent. I sat on the floor in shock. No one asked me if I was OK. No one reached out a hand to help me get back to my feet. I was terrified. I wasn't hurt but I had no idea whether the man who had pushed me to the ground was waiting for me to get up so he could have another go. I thought I sensed him standing over me. The silence of everyone else in the carriage suggested that he did not look like the kind of bloke anyone sane wanted to tangle with. I already knew from when he got in my face that he was definitely much bigger than I was.

But I couldn't just stay on the floor. I had to get up again. Thankfully, the white cane's loop was still around my wrist, so I hadn't lost it altogether. I got the cane back into my hand and used it to give myself extra stability as I slowly, slowly stood back up. My heart was pounding. The blood was rushing in my ears. The idea that so many people were just standing around me, almost certainly staring, while I was in such a helpless state was horrendous. I had never felt so vulnerable or lonely. And believe me, since losing my sight, I thought I'd felt as isolated as it was possible to be.

So I got to my feet and stood there shaking, bracing for another blow. For all I knew, my attacker might be standing right in front of me. Thankfully, he said nothing more – but neither did anyone else. Of all those dozens of people who had boarded the train at ExCel, not one asked me how I was or offered to bear witness to what had happened. At the next stop, I stumbled off the carriage onto the platform, not knowing whether my attacker was following me off the train. As quickly as I could, I got away from the edge of the platform, backed myself up against a wall and sank down onto the floor, where I wept with fear and frustration. Still no one came to ask me if I was OK. There was not a single good Samaritan to be found.

When I could finally speak again, I called Seema and together we worked out where I was. She was with me as quickly as she could be, rushing onto the platform and wrapping me in her arms in one of those hugs that could usually make everything better.

As I gave her the details of what had happened, she grew more and more furious on my behalf. It wasn't long before she was shaking with anger and upset. Why had no one helped me? Why had no one stopped the man or made a citizen's arrest? What kind of city were we living in? She wanted to call the police and make a report. There were CCTV cameras all over the DLR. It would be easy enough to find out exactly what had happened and identify my attacker. He shouldn't be allowed to get away with it.

Seema was right, of course, and perhaps we should have

followed the incident up, but I was exhausted. On a good day, getting around my complex with my white cane was nerve-wracking enough. This trip out had taken everything I had. I just wanted to go home and close the door on the outside world. From having set out that morning feeling optimistic that I was about to achieve a new level of independence, I didn't leave the house on my own again for three months.

It wasn't to be the last time I encountered the worst of humankind on the DLR. After that horrible day, I went straight back to practising walking with my cane in the safety of the complex, but my confidence was shaken and I was incredibly anxious at the thought of stepping out alone. Seema did her best to help me through my anxieties. Most evenings and every weekend, she would insist we get out there and take the Tube or DLR together. It definitely helped.

A few months later, when I was finally confident enough to use the DLR alone again, I set out on another journey to the centre. From the sound of things, I guessed I was sitting in a fairly empty carriage this time. I didn't know how many other people were in the carriage with me. Maybe two or three? Everyone was sitting silently, minding his or her own business. Except it turned out that one of the other passengers wasn't minding his own business at all. He was trying to work out what my white cane really meant.

I was utterly oblivious as this man sat down opposite me and started to wave his hands right in front of my face. When the train got to my stop and I stood up to get out, Mr Jazz Hands made to put his hand in my bag and help himself to my stuff. It was at that moment that I discovered there was a guard in the carriage. He quickly apprehended my new friend and told me what he'd seen. Mr Jazz Hands didn't get away with anything, but finding out that someone had tried to rob me was another blow to my trust in my fellow Londoners.

I now realized that before I lost my sight I'd been sheltered. There were things I'd never had to think about. There really were people out there who thought nothing of preying on the disabled. I'd been an easy target to that scumbag on the train. So I quickly learned I had to mask my vulnerability in any way I could. I couldn't get rid of my white cane, of course, but I took to carrying my bag differently, using a cross-body strap so that no one could dip into it without my knowledge. I made sure that any tech, like my phone, was safely hidden in a deep pocket unless I absolutely had to use it.

But it wasn't just on the DLR where I had to be careful. Just weeks later, I experienced equally bad behaviour on a bus.

When a bus driver stops for a person who is visually impaired, they are trained to line the bus doors up with the VIP so that they can walk straight on. When the doors are open, the driver is supposed to shout out the number of the bus and its destination. One morning, a bus driver did exactly that, but as I was boarding, I tripped and fell.

Unbelievably, while I was down on the floor, none of my fellow passengers stopped to help me. Instead, they took advantage of my fall to get ahead of me in the bus queue. One woman actually pushed her child's buggy right over me, using me like a ramp in her haste to get on board. To add insult to injury, when I finally got up, the bus driver asked sarcastically, 'Are you getting on or what?'

I got on, feeling furious.

Having experienced that kind of behaviour, it's no wonder that I was often filled with fear just at the thought of leaving our flat. Add to that the constant physical pain in my eyes that I was still experiencing every day, it's no surprise that I had sleepless nights and panic attacks. It didn't matter how positive I tried to be; every time I got close to the front door I would find myself hyperventilating, my heart racing and beads of sweat forming on my forehead. Sometimes I'd only make it just outside my complex before it hit me and I was overwhelmed – the noise of the traffic around me and the thought of getting on a train made it all worse. There were even times when I'd be glued to a spot by my anxiety and have to stand there for some time until one of the security guards noticed me while doing his rounds and walked me back home. After each setback it would take days or even weeks for me to build up the courage to try again. Each time I needed to go out, I was a complete wreck. When I got home again, I was exhausted, even when I'd had a good journey.

I got used to crying in front of my loved ones. Thankfully it was easy to be vulnerable around Seema. I could never hide anything from her. She was always ready to listen and to hold me, simply enveloping me in her kindness and love. Likewise, Mum and Dad were brilliant at letting me cry. They were still living in Guildford but visited often. I remember once breaking down in front of Dad at the end of a difficult day.

He folded me into a bear hug – just like he used to do when I was a small child – and said, 'Amit, the only reason you're doing this is because you *can* get through this.'

His words fired up the old Amit deep inside. I could get through this. I would.

8

A Lucky Break

If getting used to my white cane had its hairy and sometimes flat-out scary moments, then at least my braille training was going well.

Braille is a tactile writing system used by the visually impaired. The written letters of the alphabet are replaced by a pattern of raised dots pressed out of the page that can be read with the fingertips. Each letter is represented by a certain configuration of a maximum of six dots. Imagine an egg carton containing a maximum of six eggs in two columns of three. The letter 'A' would be represented by an egg carton containing just one egg in the upper left-hand corner. The letter 'B' would be represented by two eggs in the two upper left-hand slots. For the letter 'C', there are two eggs/dots in the top row. And so on.

In fact, I learned my braille alphabet using the kind of plastic egg container you find in the fridge door and six ping pong balls, which I moved to the correct configuration for each letter. Stella introduced me to the idea in one of our sessions at the centre in Newham. She'd used it with the children she taught in Zimbabwe. It was a brilliant idea that was easy to replicate at home.

Every day, I would memorize the pattern of a new letter

and every evening, before dinner, Seema would test me on what I had learned. She was a tough examiner but that was what I needed to get ahead. I approached learning braille just as I'd approached my university finals all those years before.

The egg box method was great when it came to getting the hang of the basics, but I soon decided that I would be able to learn even more quickly if I could type out some braille of my own. There were typewriters at the centre, of course, but I wanted one at home that I could use more often. Seema started to research braille typewriters straight away, but the cheapest one she could find online cost more than £800. That's £800 for a typewriter with just eight keys. It was way out of our budget.

We were learning that braille (and indeed, being visually impaired more generally) can be a very expensive business. Though there are some great companies out there working to make books accessible to the visually impaired, a braille version of a novel can cost in the region of £20 compared with the £4.99 paperbacks you can get in the supermarkets. There are braille books in libraries, but often they are so well used that the dots have been worn down, rendering some words all but impossible to read. For someone like me, who had been an avid reader my whole life, that was pretty frustrating.

But then, not long after we'd decided a new braille typewriter was too expensive, Seema found a second-hand one on eBay. It was selling for just £40. We snapped it up. We were the only bidders. It turned out that the seller didn't even know what it was that he was practically giving away. He said he'd had it on a living room shelf as a decorative object for years. Luckily he'd taken care of it and it still worked.

Returned to its intended purpose, that braille typewriter helped me make another huge leap forward. At its most basic, practical level, braille allowed me to read the labels on my medication. I also used my braille typewriter to make up my own labels for packaging, which was an enormous help in the kitchen and bathroom. At least now I wouldn't be mixing up the can of chickpeas with the can of baked beans.

Most people wouldn't think twice about scribbling down a shopping list or a phone number or a reminder to themselves, but I couldn't do those things after I lost my sight. My braille typewriter meant that at last I was able to write again and re-read what I had written without having to have it read out loud to me. That was great. It was another piece of my independence I was getting back.

So I mastered braille and was using my long cane daily – I now felt like I was finally making progress. With my training finished, I was invited to take another course at the Newham centre – a Living with Sight Loss course. It was specially designed by the RNIB, which is the UK's largest community of blind and partially sighted people, and would cover subjects such as everyday living, assistive technology, eye health, personal well-being and welfare rights. The idea was to bring together a group of VIPs in one room so that they could share their experiences and their top tips for an independent life. I would perhaps even make some new friends.

I signed up at once. I was keen to do everything and anything I could to get used to my new situation and make the most of it. I was especially eager to hear how other people were coping, and hopefully thriving, in similar circumstances. Maybe they would have some ideas for making the best of things that hadn't yet occurred to me. I was open to any suggestions.

There were twelve people on the course, aged between eighteen and eighty. They were all from different backgrounds and they had experienced different levels of sight loss for different reasons. They were certainly a diverse bunch but the one thing they had in common was that they all seemed to be really, really negative.

We sat in a circle and the session – and the complaints – began. 'Everyone knows me round here, I don't need your help,' one man insisted, when Nick French, the course leader, asked him what he hoped to get from the next six weeks. Meanwhile, other people were having conversations between themselves.

I couldn't believe it. My course mates challenged pretty much everything that Nick French had to say. They were all so angry. I was astonished by the way they seemed determined to find fault in everything. Nothing Nick said about the resources available to us – from emotional support and legal aid to assistive technology – seemed to appeal to them. After my first day in their company I knew that if I had to spend the whole six-week course with these people I could spiral back into a pretty negative place myself.

I was too fragile to risk that. After the incident on the DLR, it had taken me three months to regain my confidence so that I could go out alone with my white cane again. And though I found I recovered more and more quickly from each negative experience following that, I knew I still had to guard my confidence like the truly precious thing it was. I couldn't let myself slide.

I was so disappointed to find myself in a room full of people determined only to focus on the worst. It was so different from what I had expected. While I appreciated their viewpoints and understood only too well why they might find it hard to find any positives at all – I'd definitely been there myself – I knew that for my own sake I needed to be around people who were in a happier place. I needed to be with people who were as determined as I was not to be defined by being visually impaired.

When I explained the situation to Nick he said that he understood. He told me that the course was also run out of the RNIB's head office in King's Cross from time to time. Perhaps I would like to join the group there instead? I might find them better company. Of course I was up for that. The only problem was that the office was right on the other side of the city.

By now, I was used to getting myself to and from the centre in Newham. Though I didn't ever look forward to the trip exactly, I knew that I could handle it. Getting to the RNIB would mean crossing London and using one of the city's biggest and busiest stations. After some deliberation, I decided I was up for the challenge.

I practised the route to the RNIB with Stella during our session and then again with Seema one Sunday afternoon, well ahead of the day the course was due to start. The practice was essential. King's Cross has six Underground lines passing through it and direct links to three airports, as well as connecting to St Pancras station, which is the Eurostar terminal. The number of people passing through the station daily terrified me. I used to get lost there before I lost my sight, as do many people, given the number of exits it has.

Seema walked me through the station – which had been so familiar to me in my past life working nearby as a sighted A&E doctor – and we worked out which exit I needed to give me the most direct path to the RNIB office. From the correct exit it was a short walk, with only one big road to cross. After Seema and I had walked from the station to the office a couple of times together, I was confident that I'd be able to white cane it on my own.

On the morning the new course began, Seema went into work as usual. Meanwhile, I got the Tube to King's Cross alone. So far, so good. At the station, I requested assistance and a kindly member of Transport for London's staff duly walked me from the Tube to the station exit. Unfortunately, they walked me to the *wrong* exit. I knew how to get to the RNIB offices from the exit Seema and I had earmarked on our Sunday afternoon recce but, of course, since I was starting from the wrong place, it wasn't long before I was totally and utterly lost.

Realizing what must have happened when I could find none of the tactile landmarks that Seema and I had incorporated into my intended route, I tried to call the RNIB for help but couldn't get through. Frustrated and a little bit worried, I called Seema and she offered to call the RNIB herself and get them to send someone to meet me. However, I couldn't tell her where I was standing and there was no one nearby to ask.

'How are we going to work out where you are?' Seema asked.

'I don't know,' I said. But then, 'I think I can smell a Burger King . . .'

Every day since I'd lost my sight, I'd been discovering new and strange things about my body and its power to adapt. I could no longer see but my ability to tune in to my other senses was becoming heightened. Just as Stella had assured me during my long cane training, I was getting better at interpreting all the information available to me. My hearing was definitely becoming sharper. I could make a good guess at how fast a car was moving from the sound of its engine now. My sense of touch was changing as well. Having cut right back on the numbing painkillers, I could read braille quickly and easily.

And it wasn't just my hands that were more sensitive; so were my feet. I had come to appreciate the slightest difference between pairs of shoes for the effect it had on my ability to feel the tactile signals on the pavement. Even with my white cane I often checked out the safety of the environment around me by prodding at things with my toes – though this meant I got through trainers in double-quick time. So when I found a pair that I liked, that offered me a degree of sensitivity as well as the safety of good grip, I bought a dozen pairs at once. Looking smart had been so important to me as a hospital doctor, but I had to accept that trainers were now the best shoes for me; dress shoes didn't feel half as safe.

That morning, my getting lost on the way to the RNIB revealed that my sense of smell had been getting stronger too. I could actually tell the difference between fast food outlets by odour alone. As superpowers went, it wasn't like being able to fly, but right then it was invaluable.

'It's definitely a Burger King,' I told Seema. The scent of a Whopper was unmistakeable.

'Right. So you're outside a Burger King near King's Cross.' Seema believed me.

Still sitting at her desk, Seema googled 'Burger King King's Cross' and it wasn't long before she was able to figure out exactly where I must be. She told me to stay put, then called Nick at the RNIB. He immediately sent someone out to find me and bring me in.

The someone Nick sent just happened to be a deaf guy with a hearing dog. Needless to say, it took my rescuer and me a little while to make contact with each other, but eventually he linked his arm through mine and we were on our way at last.

I was totally exhausted just getting to the RNIB offices that morning and I sat through the first part of the course in a daze. Thankfully, my fellow participants were much more enthusiastic than the gang at Newham had been and their energy lifted me up. By the end of the day, though, I definitely needed a burger.

Within a few weeks, I had the easiest route from home to King's Cross and the RNIB building off by heart. Never again did I need to navigate by fast food outlets, but I did long to be able to travel further afield.

When Seema had to travel to Washington DC for work, it seemed like the perfect opportunity for me to stretch my wings. Rather than stay home alone, I would tag along and we'd add a few days to her trip to visit family in New York and Toronto. The US and Canada are much like here in terms of accessibility, with distinct pavements, tactile paving and accessible pedestrian crossings for the visually impaired. Given my new-found confidence with my white cane, I thought I would be comfortable getting around while Seema worked, even if I only got as far as the nearest coffee shop. It had been such a long time since I'd flown and I had a lot of air miles just sitting there, so I decided to cash them in.

I hadn't flown at all since losing my sight and I wondered how I would cope. Luckily I had enough air miles to book a business class ticket so I was relatively sure I'd be comfortable during the flight itself, but being completely new to air travel as a blind person, I had no real idea what to expect.

The trip to the airport and getting through security went smoothly. We didn't know about the fact that special assistance was available – we just carried on as normal, with Seema guiding me on one side and my white cane extended in my other hand. Holding the cane while you're being guided might seem a bit unnecessary, but I kept getting shoulder-barged as I wasn't able to move out of the way of oncoming people quickly enough. At least this gave them early warning that I wasn't in their way out of choice but rather because I couldn't see them! So in this fashion we boarded the plane, found our seats and settled down for the eight-hour flight.

My worries prior to getting on the plane were mainly about how my eyes might cope with the air pressure in the cabin and the recycled air. I didn't want to wear sunglasses on the flight, though they might have made me more comfortable, as then not everyone would know I was blind. I'd had previous experience of people making judgemental or sarcastic comments when they didn't realize my circumstances. But in the end, the biggest problem I faced on that first flight was somewhat unexpected.

It's always the case that you don't know what you don't know, and so it was when, midway through our night flight, I woke up needing to use the bathroom. I didn't know where it was and I didn't want to wake Seema, who was fast asleep, but I couldn't find the call button for the cabin crew either. In fact, I couldn't find any buttons at all. The beautifully designed business class seats had very stylish touch buttons that were not tactile in the slightest. I was completely lost. It turned out that despite my white cane and the fact that we had advised the airline before travel that I was visually impaired, the cabin crew were oblivious to my needs. I was stuck in my seat with my legs crossed. Needless to say, it was a very long and uncomfortable flight.

On reaching Washington DC, I made a complaint to the airline. It was only then that I found out that I should have received a personal safety briefing prior to take-off. Another lesson learned for next time.

At least we had a fun time in DC – in between Seema's work, we managed to catch up with friends, eat our body-weight in oysters and check out one of the Obamas' favourite Mexican restaurants (Oyamel, FYI, if you're ever in DC). And it was a real treat to be able to surprise Seema's family in Toronto for her aunt's birthday.

A couple of months later, we decided to try flying again. On Valentine's Day 2015, we booked a spur-of-the-moment trip to India. That's not to say we hadn't thought about it and discussed it previously, but that was the day we decided to just do it. We hadn't had time to take a honeymoon right after our wedding, though we'd assumed that one day we'd get round to it. But then Seema changed jobs. And then I lost my sight.

I wanted to see my maternal family in India and desperately wanted Seema to meet them too, especially as my grandma was already quite elderly and we worried every monsoon season in particular about her health. That Valentine's Day we realized we had two options. Either we went ASAP or we had to wait until after the monsoon, which would essentially mean waiting until the end of the year. So we decided to go for it. It was likely to be above forty degrees for most of the trip, but we didn't plan to do too much – a few days relaxing in Mumbai and a visit to my grandma to spend some quality time with her before heading down to Goa for a proper rest.

As soon as we made the decision, Seema threw herself into the planning, booking flights and schedules with great enthusiasm. It would mainly be new for her, as my family lived in a different part of India to her family, but for me it would be like going home. I'd be revisiting some of my best childhood and adult memories, not to mention some of my favourite food.

Given my experience on the way to the US, the thought of the long flight was nerve-wracking and I wondered how I would cope. Unfortunately the cabin crew weren't especially helpful. We had to change planes in Dubai and requested special assistance in advance as per the advice. This was where wires got crossed.

When the time came to disembark from our flight from London, we were told we had to wait for a wheelchair. I didn't need a wheelchair. We certainly hadn't asked for one. But as far as the crew were concerned, special assistance meant a wheelchair and I wasn't getting off that plane until we had one. The wheelchair did not turn up and the cabin crew grew increasingly impatient at us for holding them up. Eventually Seema and I left the plane without any help. It was deeply frustrating that the airline assumed anyone requiring assistance was, as a default, in need of a wheelchair and it wasn't an option to have the help without the wheels. They wouldn't listen to me or recognize that I could walk.

At last we landed in the bustling city of Mumbai and jumped straight into the car sent by the Marriott hotel that Seema had so sensibly organized. Feeling grubby after the long journey, shortly after we checked in I decided I wanted a shave. You can get a great shave in India. I went to a nearby barber's and put my trust in the man with the razor. But I could tell pretty soon that something wasn't quite right. The razor felt shorter than I expected and wasn't very smooth on my skin. Seema confirmed that the barber had tried to get away with giving me a shave with a rusty old plastic Bic, thinking because I couldn't see it wouldn't matter. There was nothing I disliked more than feeling that someone was willing to take advantage of my blindness. Luckily, the barber was in the minority.

We hadn't told my grandma that we were coming to see her. My parents were going to be in India at the same time but we'd convinced them to keep our trip a surprise – something that is incredibly difficult for my mum, as she is not

Me, aged four, with my younger brother Mital and
our parents shortly before we moved to Guildford.

Growing up, Diwali was my
favourite time of the year.

Rain never stopped play. I was
100 per cent committed to whatever
sport I was into at the time and broke
a few vases along the way.

ABOVE LEFT I spent many happy hours tinkering with the flight simulator at the ATC in the hope of getting it working. ABOVE RIGHT My first taste of scrubs and a white coat. To say that I was nervous is putting it mildly. BELOW The thing I loved most about being in India was the people I got to meet out there.

ABOVE Cornwall will always be our happy place. Summer was over, but we still had champagne and pasties on the beach! BELOW Our Indian engagement ceremony was the start of our happily ever after. I think our faces say it all – we were just so content to be together.

Our big fat Indian wedding. One of the symbols of a married woman is red powder in the parting of her hair and that's what I'm applying here.

My first trip to India after losing my sight. Seema and I finally managed to take a belated honeymoon in Goa.

Kika as a tiny puppy, only four months old.
Wasn't she just adorable?

Puppy Kika's penchant for
muddy puddles knew no bounds!

An eighteen-month-old Kika and her German shepherd
trainee guide dog buddy in Westminster.

Meeting Beau, a confident pup-in-training, who I really clicked with.

The first time I met Kika. I think I was more nervous than she was.

ABOVE While training at Redbridge, Kika would wake me up in the morning with a deep sigh, resting her head on the bed next to me!

RIGHT Learning how to look after Kika properly – this included grooming her.

BELOW Kika stayed with me in my hotel room throughout our training. She's always been unconventional in her approach to sleep . . .

Learning how to cross roads safely with Kika.

Kika settled into her new home with Seema and me very quickly.
She was always on the rug and had no shortage of toys.

good with secrets – and arranged for them to pick us up at Indore Airport. When the moment came, they told my grandmother that some family friends were coming to visit for a few days, which was enough to persuade her into the car for the three-hour drive to meet our flight.

Walking out of the airport back into the heat and the noise was an assault on the senses. I clutched Seema's arm as we made our way out to the crowd, looking for Mum and Dad in the sea of people. I may not have been able to see her face, but I knew my grandma was smiling when she saw me again after so long. I felt her tears of joy when I hugged her. She clung on to me for what felt like ages, until she realized that Seema was by my side. Since my grandma had been unable to travel to our wedding, it was the first time these two wonderful women had met and both were delighted to be together at last.

Once we reached my grandma's house, I was able to relax. Grandma had taken my sight loss as quite the shock, but her being able to hug me and see me in the flesh somehow made everything better for both of us. The country air, the fresh food, the familial comforts all made up for the searing forty-five-degree heat and the mosquito bites. With no air con and no electricity most evenings, we really were back to the simple life, but I loved every second of it. Our days were spent chatting with my grandma, uncle, aunt and cousins, visiting the local temple, shopping in the markets for groceries (of course my grandma and aunt were making all my favourite dishes) and generally taking it very easy.

The hardest part was, as always, navigating away from home. Unlike in the UK, there's no tactile paving in rural

India to help the visually impaired find their way around. Indeed, there was little in terms of consistent pavement, crossings and traffic signals and instead lots of street clutter, rubbish and makeshift stalls that popped up in different places from day to day. Combined with the intense heat and constant noise from car and truck horns beeping, it made for a blind person's worst nightmare – total sensory overload.

A white cane would have been useless in such a situation so I reverted to what I knew best – Seema taking my arm and walking and talking me through everything. This was how we had coped when I first lost my sight. Looking at us, you'd have seen a couple arm in arm, strolling along together. What you might not have noticed was Seema whispering in my ear as we walked, giving an audio description of everything around me. She'd become an expert at painting a verbal picture of our surroundings, describing the state of the paving ahead, nearby landmarks and even the physical characteristics of anyone that approached us. Luckily I still remembered key places well, so when she mentioned that we were approaching the neighbouring school, for example, I asked if the tea stall was still outside. This is how we navigated around the bustling streets of India – arm in arm, side by side.

Given all the travelling we were doing in India, we took a fair few internal flights. The concerns we'd had when travelling in the UK and US were amplified as we had no idea of what level of service to expect or how accessible smaller airports and airlines would be. We needn't have worried. We have never been better looked after than we were when flying within India. From check-in to boarding the plane and the on-flight experience, the assistance was flawless. At every airport we had a single person escort us to the plane and the same in reverse at the other end of the flight. At no point was Seema left struggling to pull bags off the luggage belt alone as she usually is in the UK. There was no battle for help getting through security. We were even allowed to check in our carry-on bags so we didn't have to worry about carrying them through the airport and on board the plane. This all reduced the pressure on us massively. It's the little things that make the biggest difference.

After everything we'd been through, we were like giddy schoolchildren as soon as we got on the plane to Goa for the final leg of our trip – chatty and excited, giggling away about our plans to eat excessive amounts of seafood. We'd booked a cabin on the beach for ten days. Just the two of us. Making the trip felt like another step forward, getting back to who we were as a couple.

On the flight – which was full of honeymooners – a member of the cabin crew commented on how happy Seema and I looked together. 'More like best friends than husband and wife!' she said. We laughed at that. But we came to understand what she meant. None of the honeymooning passengers seemed to be talking to each other – possibly some of them were in arranged marriages and didn't actually know each other that well. In contrast, Seema and I were chatting away because we were best friends *and* husband and wife. The past year and a half, which might well have torn us apart, had instead made us realize just what an unshakeable bond we had. We'd honoured the promises we made to each other in the Marylebone registry office and reaffirmed at our big fat Indian wedding again and again and again.

That blissful holiday in Goa gave us a chance to reflect on all that we'd been through since that awful November day in 2013 and marvel that we'd made it so far. Though we knew there was still a long way to go before I completely regained my independence, we allowed ourselves to hope that the worst was already behind us and there was much to look forward to.

While we were in India, Seema and I talked seriously for the first time about the possibility of my getting a guide dog. Pauline Acott at the centre for the visually impaired in Newham had suggested to me that I could be a suitable candidate, and Seema had been turning the idea over in her mind ever since.

Shortly before we booked our trip, I'd gone through that awful experience at King's Cross when the teenage prankster spun me around and left me unable to tell where I was standing on a packed Tube platform. It had worked out OK in the end – a fellow commuter had seen what had happened and helped me reorient myself and get onto the next train – but it was still worrying to have found myself so vulnerable. Seema suggested that if I'd had a guide dog by my side, the teenage joker wouldn't have been so brave. Similarly, opportunists like the thief on the DLR might be discouraged from getting too close. It was an interesting idea, but getting a guide dog still seemed like something we weren't quite ready for. At least, I wasn't quite ready for it. We'd experienced so many changes in such a short time, I reasoned. We needed a rest. 'Maybe in a little while,' I said.

Our impromptu trip to India had surprised and delighted us. We returned from our holiday feeling happy and re-energized and ready to face London life again.

9

A Puppy Playdate

Back in the UK, Seema was keen to learn more about guide dogs and threw herself into volunteering at the Guide Dogs for the Blind Association's headquarters on the Euston Road. She learned how to properly guide the visually impaired through their 'My Guide' training course. She also wanted to know more about the reality of life with an assistance animal.

One afternoon, I was catching up with friends from the Living with Sight Loss course. My confusing first trip to the RNIB office in King's Cross had been more than worth it – I'd been delighted to meet a much more positive group of people there after the disappointment of the Newham course. We'd stayed in touch and met up regularly for lunch and a chat.

Each month, one person would be tasked with organizing our get-together, choosing a place close to them. The rest of us would meet at the nearest station and walk the last leg of the journey together. It was often a challenge to get to different, unknown parts of London but was always well worth it. It helped build my confidence travelling across London solo. More importantly, it was great to have a new social circle who understood my life, because the sad fact was, when I lost my sight, I lost a lot of old friends too. It seemed they just didn't know what to say to me. At first they called to see how I was getting on, but gradually those calls had become less frequent until they stopped altogether. It was very lonely.

Anyway, that day, I was actually at the RNIB with my new friends when Seema phoned to ask if I could meet her at Guide Dogs' London office, where she was attending a volunteer get-together. Since it wasn't somewhere I'd visited at that point, I was a little nervous about getting there, but I knew the area from having worked there during my A&E days and could still picture where I would need to go. The route between the RNIB and Guide Dogs on the Euston Road was basically one straight line. I decided I could white cane it alone, though I might need a little assistance at some of the crossings on the way.

The walk went well. I seemed to find help whenever I needed it and I made it to the Guide Dogs office much more quickly than I'd expected to. After that easy journey, I felt calm and relaxed as I arrived. Someone met me at the door and offered to take me to the fourth floor where Seema was waiting for me.

'You're in for a treat,' he said. At this point, I still wasn't entirely sure why Seema wanted me to meet her there. When my new friend told me I was 'in for a treat', I was probably thinking, *There must be cake*. But the fourth floor of the office I was taken to was unlike any office I'd ever been in. On the way up, I was told that each desk had its very own puppy pen around it and, that day, the pens were full of puppies.

The first thing that struck me as I walked into the room

was the smell. That unique puppy smell. Then there was the noise! The barking. The whining. The squeaking. The yelps of indignation and excitement as they tumbled over each other at play. I stood at the door wondering what on earth I was about to walk into.

'Lots of puppies in here,' my new friend told me, slightly unnecessarily.

'I can hear them!'

I was greeted by Dave Kent, Guide Dogs' London engagement officer. A big softly spoken Welsh guy, Dave has been visually impaired from birth. We clicked at once. Then Dave suggested he join Seema and me for a conversation about the dogs. 'Maybe you've got some questions,' he said.

I had loads of questions, as by now I'd cottoned on to why Seema had asked me to be there.

A couple of minutes later, Dave, Seema and I were sitting on the floor in a pen, with puppies crawling all over us. At one point, I had three dogs licking my face. Their excitement was infectious and any anxieties I had evaporated. Having the pups around made it easy somehow. Since losing my sight and gaining a cane, I often felt like I was the centre of attention whenever I walked into a room, even if I couldn't see people staring. At the same time, the very thing that made me stand out also isolated me. People were nervous of my sight loss and didn't know how to talk to me. Conversations with new people could be difficult but this was different. The puppies provided another point of focus. I just enjoyed the craziness of the experience. The smell, the soft fur, the yapping. It was hard to believe that these anarchic bundles of fluff would one day be assistance animals.

Dave assured us that these puppies were the cream of the crop. They'd already passed a great many tests to get to this stage. They'd been bred from parents carefully chosen for temperament and intelligence, then constantly assessed from birth to see if they were developing the right qualities to be a guide dog. How was their ability to handle noise? Distractions? Could they focus? Were they able to pick new skills up quickly? Though they seemed completely bonkers, they would grow up to be as calm, serene and sensible as the adult guide dogs I'd seen in the past. For now, though, a long training journey lay ahead of them.

What struck me immediately about Dave was that, unlike most people, he focused a lot of his attention on Seema that day. He asked her how she was getting on and how she was feeling. I could tell from Seema's slightly hesitant answers that she was surprised but pleased to be asked (while unsure how to respond) and I was reminded once again of how hard living with my sight loss was for *both* of us.

The puppies were like furry therapists as we spoke about what a shock my going blind had been and how we'd got this far. As all our hopes and fears poured out in one long stream, Dave listened with compassion and understanding. I think I already knew at this first meeting that he would turn out to be a good friend.

We played with the puppies for an hour or so before it was time to go home. Seema was delighted by the whole experience. So was I. As we left the building, she said, 'You know you've got a great big smile on your face?' I could tell from her voice that she was grinning too. She linked her arm through mine and we walked to the Tube.

'So, how do you feel?' she asked when we got back home. 'I mean about maybe getting a guide dog of your own?'

How did I feel? I had certainly enjoyed meeting the puppies, but beyond that? It was a big question and I knew it wasn't as simple as saying, 'Yes, I'd like a dog now, please.'

I answered cautiously. 'Seema, a person doesn't just "get" a guide dog and then have everything magically fall into place. I mean, it's a dog after all. A creature with a mind of its own.'

We all know what dogs are like – happy, loving and care-free. Most dog owners I know also describe their dogs as being a little bit *crazy*. Even the best-trained dogs will go nuts for a ball or a stick or a chance to chase the neighbours' cat. They'd snaffle anything vaguely edible, shred anything they couldn't eat, jump into any filthy pool of water they could find and dry off on their owner's favourite chair.

'The difference between a guide dog and a white cane is more than dealing with feeding and pooping,' I told Seema. 'With a cane, you're one hundred per cent in control . . .'

I knew myself well enough to know that I liked the feeling of being a hundred per cent in control. With a white cane you make all the decisions and you can only blame yourself if something goes wrong. A white cane is never going to be distracted by a doughnut. It's never going to drag you across four lanes of traffic in pursuit of a squirrel. It's never going to bite someone. It can't get hurt if you cross the road at the wrong time.

Knowing all of this, how could I put my life in a dog's paws?

All the same, I had enjoyed meeting those puppies and Dave's story had gone a long way to convincing me that his life was much better for having his own guide dog, Chad, a Labrador-retriever cross. Dave and Chad had only recently been matched to each other and started working together after the retirement of Chad's predecessor, Quince. Chad was, in fact, Dave's ninth guide dog, so while Dave would never have pushed having a guide dog on anyone, he was definitely able to vouch for the positive effect it could have.

So despite my long list of reasons why it was a ridiculous idea, just a couple of days later I agreed with Seema that we should at least give the idea of my getting a guide dog some serious thought.

The decision to get a guide dog could ultimately only be mine – it would be an enormous commitment requiring a great deal of work on my part – but I knew Seema was ready to support me through every step of the process if I wanted to go for it. I was grateful for her attention to detail as she looked deeper into the practicalities.

Seema wasn't taking the idea of my getting a guide dog lightly by any means. She had grown up very nervous of big dogs, having been bitten by a German shepherd at the age of four. However, Dave had been brilliant at addressing Seema's fears. He'd assured her that if someone in a VIP's family has an issue with dogs, you could start by specifying a particular breed.

The breed of dog most closely associated with guide dogs is the Labrador, but the charity also trains golden retrievers, German shepherds, retriever crosses and Labradoodles to name but a few. The Labradoodles – poodles crossed with Labradors – are great for people with allergies because they don't shed their fur. Dave explained to us that some City workers ask for Labradoodles or black Labradors so they won't have to go to work in a dark suit covered in blond dog hair! It was reassuring to hear about all the different things that are taken into account when matching a guide dog with a new owner. Allergies, other pets already in the house, the local environment and the sort of journeys the dog and owner will have to make every day are all thrown into the equation.

In the weeks following our first puppy playdate, we continued to investigate the process of getting a dog. Seema met other guide dog owners and staff from the charity through her volunteer training and heard first-hand what the benefits would be for me and for us as a couple. But I was still hesitating, going backwards and forwards on the matter like a pendulum. It seemed fraught with risk. Sure, there were limitations to life with a white cane, but there wasn't anything like the same possibility for complete and total catastrophe that could come from relying so utterly on an animal just a few generations removed from a wolf. Was it really possible to train a dog so well that I could trust it with my life?

10

Man's Best Friend

I first became aware of guide dogs when I was a child. My parents kept a Labrador-shaped collection tin for the Guide Dogs for the Blind Association on the counter next to the till in their shop. Though I didn't meet any guide dogs while I was growing up, I also had a little bit of knowledge about them from *Blue Peter*, the children's TV programme, which often ran fund-raising campaigns for the charity, asking viewers to send in used stamps, milk bottle tops and aluminium foil to be converted into cash to support a pup through its expensive training.

Now that a guide dog might be in my own future, I wanted to know more about their history. I soon discovered that they've been around for centuries. What is believed to be the earliest known representation of a visually impaired person using an assistance dog can be found in a first century AD mural in the ancient Roman city of Herculaneum, which was destroyed in the same volcanic eruption that buried Pompeii. The two-thousand-year-old wall painting shows a raggedly dressed man begging for alms. He carries a staff, thought to represent his blindness, but he also has a small dog on a lead. That the man and his dog made it onto a mural suggests there was something very special about their partnership.

It's likely that dogs have been used as assistance animals ever since then. They've been found depicted in a thirteenth-century Chinese scroll painting. In the 1600s, the famous painter Rembrandt made sketches of a local blind man and his dog. The formal training of guide dogs, however, only began in earnest in the eighteenth century, in Paris, at the Hospice des Quinze-Vingts, a hospital dedicated to the care of the blind.

In the nineteenth century, Johann Wilhelm Klein, founder of Vienna's Institute for the Education of the Blind, wrote a manual on education for the visually impaired, which included his ideas on guide dog training. Klein was the first to suggest that swapping a soft lead for a stiff harness could mean the person walking the dog was better able to interpret the dog's movements.

A hundred years later, during the First World War, guide dogs were trained to support soldiers blinded by poisonous gas in the trenches. In 1916, Gerhard Stalling opened the world's first official guide dog training school in Oldenburg, Germany, motivated by the way his own dog was instinctively protective of a young blind patient.

Dr Stalling's schools spread his ideas around the world. He inspired American guide dog pioneer Dorothy Harrison Eustis, who began training dogs of her own in the 1920s. Her first successful match was between a young man called Morris Frank and a German shepherd called Buddy. Frank and Buddy became celebrities when hundreds watched in awe as Buddy navigated Frank across New York's West Street, which was locally known as 'Death Avenue'. This dangerous feat encouraged New Yorkers to support Frank and Eustis in the 1929 foundation of The Seeing Eye, America's first guide dog training organization.

In the United Kingdom, the equivalent British charity, the Guide Dogs for the Blind Association – known to me simply as 'Guide Dogs' – began five years later in 1931. Encouraged by the feats of Frank and Buddy, Muriel Crooke and Rosamund Bond, who were both German shepherd breeders, trained the first four British guide dogs from a makeshift base in a lock-up garage in Merseyside.

Those first four dogs were called Flash, Folly, Judy and Meta and they were a big success when they were matched with four blind men. Two years later, Crooke and Bond were joined by experienced Russian guide dog trainer Captain Nikolai Liakhoff, who had worked at The Seeing Eye, and the Guide Dogs organization was officially born. The training centre moved from the lock-up garage to much grander premises at The Cliff in Wallasey. It remained there until 1941, when The Cliff building was commandeered for the war effort and the charity moved to Leamington Spa.

Post-war, the charity expanded rapidly. In the 1950s, the first volunteer puppy walkers were recruited – these are people who look after the pups in their own homes to help socialize them ahead of training – and Guide Dogs began its own breeding programme. In the sixties, the charity's work was brought to the attention of a whole new generation of supporters when *Blue Peter* dedicated its 1964 Christmas appeal to raising money to fund the show's first guide dog puppies.

That year, Blue Peter viewers collected enough milk bottle tops and discarded silver foil to pay for the training of two pups, named Cindy and Honey. Blue Peter has since sponsored a number of guide dogs.

These days, Guide Dogs' head office is in Reading in Berkshire. There are regional offices all over the country. There are also four official Guide Dogs training schools at Leamington Spa, Redbridge, Atherton and Forfar. Leamington Spa is still home to the charity's breeding centre. Guide Dogs breeds around 1,300 puppies each year and there are now more than 5,000 guide dog owners in the United Kingdom. High-profile owners include Paralympian Libby Clegg and politician David Blunkett. Since the 1930s, Guide Dogs have changed countless lives. Not bad for an organization that started life in someone's garage.

All those years of trial and error by so many guide dog pioneers have resulted in the development of a modern training regime that is the equivalent of attending a canine university. The process begins before the future guide dogs are even born, when the breeding centre at Leamington Spa matches adult dogs in the hope of creating a litter of puppies with the right personality for the job. Guide dog puppies are usually born in volunteers' homes, where they live with their mother for the first few weeks of their lives. When the puppies are six weeks old and weaned, they go to the centre at Leamington Spa, where they are vaccinated and microchipped and checked for fitness and suitability of temperament. Then they'll be matched with the volunteer 'puppy walkers' who will look after them for the next fourteen months. These volunteers live all over the country and in all sorts of situations. Many have young families, who help get the puppies used to the rough and tumble of living with children. Guide Dogs are always looking for puppy walkers.

The puppy walkers have an important job ahead when they

take on one of Guide Dogs' pups. Training any puppy is hard work, but when it comes to junior guide dogs, the stakes are even higher. The puppies need to be housetrained to begin with. After two months or so, once they've received their booster vaccinations, the puppies are allowed out into the big wide world for the first time, wearing a blue puppy jacket emblazoned with the words 'Guide Dog Puppy in Training'. This is when they can start to socialize and get used to walking on the lead. It's too early to learn guiding commands, but they do need to learn all the basic commands, such as 'sit' and 'down', 'walk on' and 'let's go', at this stage. Table manners are also important. At meal times, the puppies are taught to wait for a whistle before they start eating. They need to be introduced to travelling on buses and trains too.

There is a lot to learn. A puppy training supervisor supports the volunteers throughout the process and the puppies' progress is assessed every six months. A dog that isn't progressing as it should be may be rehomed with a more experienced puppy walker to see if that makes a difference. If, after that, a puppy still isn't showing the aptitude it will need to complete its training, it will be found a permanent home where it can live as a pet. Fortunately, there is a long waiting list of dog lovers waiting to give a home to guide dog school dropouts.

When the successful puppies are between fourteen and eighteen months old, they are returned to their designated Guide Dogs training centre to begin learning all their important guiding skills. It's an emotional moment – for the puppy walkers at least. I've been assured by the guide dog trainers I've spoken to that the puppy walkers miss their charges far more than the other way round! There are always tears from the volunteers when the puppies are handed over. The puppies are just excited to be in a new environment and to have new friends to play with and bound off without a backward glance.

The next stage, known as 'early training', takes four months and focuses on obedience skills. Some of the dogs live at the centre for the duration while others are 'boarders', living with local families and being picked up and dropped off every day on a sort of doggy school run.

When they're at school, the new recruits swap their puppy jackets for proper harnesses, officially declaring them 'Guide Dogs in Training'. The first four weeks are about finding out what the puppies are capable of and what they can cope with. They're taught how to walk down the street safely, which means sticking to the middle of the pavement, stopping at kerbs and only changing direction when the handler says so. Of course, the guide dog puppies are just like any dogs and they need incentives to learn all these new skills. They're encouraged with tasty treats, which come out of their daily food allowance. The harder the skill – or the more resistant the puppy seems to be to learning that skill – the tastier the reward. For tastier, read smellier, as I would discover in due course.

At the end of the working day, the puppies are given plenty of time to socialize and play before they have their evening meal in the kennels or their doggy foster families pick them up for the night. Training takes place over five days a week and the pups always have the weekends off. At Redbridge, there are big fields where the pups can run free when school's out.

The trainee guide dogs are continually assessed and, even at this stage, not all will go on to be matched with a visually impaired owner. However, if they're not successful, the training won't have been a waste of time by any means. All assistance dogs have to pass the same initial test – the public access test, which among other things assesses a dog's ability to follow basic commands and interact safely with the public – before they go on to specialist training that will match their skills to their future owner's needs. Often guide dog trainees who don't make the grade go on to have great careers as hearing dogs, sniffer dogs or emotional support dogs known as 'buddy dogs'.

After four months, trainees who do make the grade now begin their advanced training with a guide dog mobility instructor, who trains them to guide a visually impaired person and also teaches the VIP how to work with and look after the dog. This is when the real alchemy takes place, as the advanced trainers get to know their charges and work out what sort of owner each dog would suit. Just like people, dogs have very different personalities and preferences. A prospective guide dog owner living in a village needs a dog with an entirely different profile from a prospective owner living in London. Now is also the time when the dogs learn more specific skills such as travelling on escalators.

The graduates of the Guide Dogs training scheme are the assistance animal elite. Little by little, I was coming to understand that being a guide dog owner is an enormous privilege.

11

A Star is Born

On the other side of the country, another part of this story was unfolding.

On 14 November 2013, a beautiful female yellow Labrador puppy was born to one of Guide Dogs' specially chosen breeding pairs. She was christened Kika and she was a perfect bundle of bright furry joy.

As soon as she was weaned, chipped and vaccinated, Kika was homed with her puppy walker Lucy and Lucy's six-year-old daughter. They fell in love with her at once. From the very beginning she had a larger than life personality. Though she looked good as gold with her soft brown eyes and enchanting doggy smile, she had a naughty streak as wide as the Thames.

Lucy told me all about it in a letter. 'The first guide dog pup we had was lovely, he was really well behaved, he never stole anything and always did as he was told – Kika was a whole different story! She used to steal anything she could get her tiny teeth on – my daughter's clothes and shoes were favourites – though she never chewed anything, just took the stuff into her bed and kept it for herself.'

She added, 'Stones were her favourite thing to play with. They were really great if they got "accidentally" dropped in dirty puddles and rivers. She honestly used to sniff out the muddiest puddle she could possibly find. She'd dig around in it for a while, looking for stones, leaves or twigs. Then she'd lie down in it! She also loved long wet grass. She'd run around and rub herself in it for ages. Basically, she was a very wet and muddy puppy most of the time.'

But despite her naughty streak, Lucy found, 'Kika was always very entertaining, extremely playful and always full of beans. She was also very caring, sociable and loveable.'

Which hopefully made up for the fact that Kika also had a penchant for tearing great tufts of grass out of Lucy's mum's pristine lawn.

Unfortunately, though, after five months, Lucy and her family faced a change of circumstances and couldn't look after Kika any longer, so she was sent to a second puppy walker, Andrea, who lived near Reading.

Remembering Kika's puppy days, Andrea told me, 'After a few days with us, she calmed down and quickly settled in. She became part of our family, with two girls aged eleven and fourteen and a couple of chickens. Kika slotted into our family routine almost straight away, attending after-school clubs with me, school Guide Dogs charity fêtes, regular visits on buses and trains. She attended weekly guide dog puppy classes and even enjoyed a visit to the local swimming pool. With each event her confidence grew and it was a pleasure to take her anywhere, from family visits to the weekly food shop. She always enjoyed her walks and couldn't resist ploughing through muddy puddles nose first on her free runs and then looking very pleased with herself afterwards with her face completely covered in mud!'

Mud was clearly a theme.

In February 2015, Kika returned to the Guide Dogs kennels at Redbridge to finish her puppy days there. However, by this time her big personality and intelligence were manifesting themselves as a certain wilfulness that was worrying to the puppy walking assessors. Would she settle down for training? She was fifteen months old and her future as a guide dog was in jeopardy.

Initially, Kika did not react well to another change of address. One of her trainers, Richard, recalled the first time he met her at the puppy block. She had been placed in a run where she could socialize with the other pups, but rather than throw herself into the puppy games, Richard said, 'Kika stood still as a statue,' ignoring the rough and tumble around her.

This continued for a few days. Every time she was out in the run Kika just stood in the corner, refusing to interact with anyone – canine or human. It got worse. If she was taken out of the run, she could just about be persuaded to put on her blue puppy jacket for a walk, but when Richard tried to introduce her to an adult guide dog harness, Kika would first give him side eye then simply drop to the floor and refuse to move, like a toddler throwing a tantrum about getting back into the pram. She wouldn't stand up again until the harness was taken away.

Guide dog trainer Roz Wakelin, who eventually took over Kika's care, described the harness problem to me: 'It was very dramatic. She looked like a stunt dog that had been taught to drop to the ground! She was determined not to wear it.'

Eventually, Roz – who was soon to qualify as a senior instructor – came up with a plan to get round Kika's refusal of the harness. Every time she needed to get Kika into it, she would take her for a run first, hoping to burn off some excess energy and make Kika feel appreciated. Then she would lure Kika to put her head into the harness with food. Labradors have a reputation for being particularly interested in anything edible – they simply love to eat – and Kika was no exception. After three weeks, the plan worked, although, Roz said, 'She still always did the "Kika shake" after we had set off.'

The 'Kika shake' is a full-body shake that I would come to know well. Apparently, when she was at the training centre, Kika would shake as many as twenty times in a row when she first had the harness on.

Fortunately, Roz understood what was going on. She was used to the ways trainee guide dogs express their anxiety in strange situations. Some lick their lips. Some yawn. Kika gave her shake. 'I knew after she did it she was settled and she would work fine in the harness,' Roz said. 'The shake was actually a sign of acceptance.'

There were other issues too. Roz worked alongside Pete Smith who had been with Guide Dogs for over forty years. He mentored Roz through advanced training with Kika. His initial assessment of Kika was that 'she is a very scent-orientated dog'.

'In other words, her nose was always stuck to the ground or the odd lamp post, which Pete found most frustrating!' Roz explained. 'She was more like a bloodhound than a Labrador.' At the same time, Kika was very intelligent and quick to pick things up. Especially if there was a tasty treat on offer. It seemed things just had to be on her terms.

It took six weeks for Roz to feel like she and Kika had a

strong enough bond to finish her training, which proceeded with lots of bribery and changing things up to keep it interesting. Even then, Roz suspected that Kika was going to be a tricky dog to place.

Where would they find an owner who could keep Kika as fully engaged as she needed to be, day after day? Kika had to be on the go all the time to be happy. Who would have the energy to keep up with her? She'd never be content with one walk a day. And who would be able to cope with her 'Kika-isms', as Roz had come to call them? The 'Kika shake' and her devotion to smelling her way through the world. Was there a VIP out there who could take Kika on and help her thrive? Or would all the hard work Roz and the other trainers had put into this funny, cheeky dog come to nothing?

12

The Perfect Match

Back in London, I was undergoing my own series of tests. After a month or so of going back and forth, Seema and I had decided we were ready to take the plunge and made our formal application for a guide dog. The first stage in the process was a home visit from the people at Guide Dogs to see how Seema and I lived and whether our situation was actually suitable for a dog. We hoped it would be. We were in a flat but it was on the first floor, with patio doors that opened directly onto a raised terrace so large you could have held a festival out there. It was safe and secure and the whole complex was gated with a key entry system.

Strictly speaking, no pets were allowed where we lived, but an assistance dog would be a different matter. There are strict rules that stop landlords refusing them. Fortunately, the management in our building were a hundred per cent behind our decision to apply for a guide dog. I already had a good rapport with the security team and they seemed almost as excited as we were at the prospect of a canine addition to the building's residents. They'd watched me struggle through my white cane training. They knew how much it meant to me to be able to get around on my own and understood how a dog would open up my life even more. They assured me they would do whatever they could to help.

In the run-up to that first meeting, Seema and I did everything we could to ensure that the Guide Dogs assessors would be impressed by our home. The flat was immaculate. We made sure there were no trip hazards and that there was plenty of room for our important visitors to get about. I also practised making everything I did – such as getting from room to room or making the tea – look absolutely effortless, so the assessors would be convinced that however difficult guide dog training would be, I could handle it.

I'd fallen back on my old ATC training with Warrant Officer Wachtel to streamline my home routines. It was all about good planning. So long as everything was in its proper place and went back in that place after I'd finished with it, I could navigate my way around the flat, prepare drinks and be the perfect host with no problems.

On the day of the assessment itself, Seema was at work and I was home alone when the Guide Dogs assessor and a couple of trainees arrived. The chief assessor was a chap called David, who was a guide dog mobility instructor. He was being shadowed by Tommy, who was soon to qualify as a GDMI himself. Tommy was from Preston. The fact that I knew Preston well, thanks to Seema and her family, helped us to quickly find common ground and went some way to putting me at ease.

'We want our guide dog owners to be confident even before they get a match,' David said. 'You still need to be able to go out independently in case there is ever a day when the dog can't work.'

I hoped that my proficiency with the white cane would convince him of that.

David also explained that I would need to work out several routes around the neighbourhood for days when I wasn't planning to go out for a specific reason because, of course, the dog would need to go out every day to get some exercise regardless of my schedule.

After I'd successfully made everyone a cup of tea, we settled on the sofas and, as you can imagine, in order to further assess my suitability as a guide dog owner, David and his colleagues asked a lot of personal questions. They'd checked out the flat and my ability to get around, now they wanted to know everything about my sight loss journey so far. How had I handled the change in my circumstances? How was I dealing with the psychological impact as well as the practicalities? How about Seema? Did she really want me to get a dog? They also wanted to know about my hopes for the future. One of the hardest questions to answer was, 'Do you want to have children?'

When I met Seema and we fell in love and got married, children were right at the centre of our plans for the future. I couldn't think of anything better than having a family with the love of my life. Since I'd lost my sight, though, things were different. I had spent the last eighteen months learning how to be something like an independent adult again. I'd mastered the art of making tea without scalding myself. I'd learned to walk with a white cane. I'd learned a whole new language in the form of braille. I was no longer too scared to leave the house alone, but the thought of raising a child, of being a hands-on dad? I wouldn't know where to start. Becoming a father still seemed like an impossible dream. I answered the question with, 'I don't know.'

Truthfully, it made me sad to even think about it.

After the initial assessment visit, I threw myself into meeting the requirements David and his colleagues had lain out. Fortunately, Stella Kamangirira, who had worked so hard to get me up and running with my white cane, jumped at the chance to help me find those all-important dog walk routes. 'When do you want to start?' she asked.

Over the next month, we came up with three forty-five-minute routes. Since I lived close to the biggest Tesco in Europe, Stella devised one dog-walking route encompassing a trip there. Previously, I'd been afraid to go there alone with my white cane because I needed to cross an enormous retail complex and its car park in order to find the pavement and my way into the shop. But now, I could go to the supermarket. That meant more to me than you can know.

Thanks to Stella, I quickly learned the routes and was assessed on them by David and Tony Wakelin, who was the husband of Roz, Kika's trainer (though I still didn't know anything about Kika yet). When I took David and Tony out, I tried to make it obvious that I was following white cane etiquette to the letter, not allowing bad habits like occasionally forgetting to swipe my cane to let me down. David told me to relax. It wasn't like a driving test where I'd get penalized for not driving with my hands at 'ten to two'. I passed the initial assessment.

The next stage was learning how to walk holding on to a harness but, of course, I couldn't train with a harness attached to a dog. Not yet. This time Becca Gamble, a guide dog mobility instructor from the London office, came to visit. She was down to earth and had a great sense of humour, which ended up being a good thing! Because I couldn't practise harness walking with a real animal for the moment, Becca had to pretend to be the dog. I held the harness handle and she held the harness. It was Becca's job to teach me the commands to which guide dogs are trained to respond. We must have made a funny sight as we paraded around the complex, with me issuing instructions such as 'let's go' and 'walk on' every time we stopped at a kerb.

At the beginning of May 2015, Becca called to invite me to an extended assessment session, which would take place over two days with an overnight stay at a hotel in between. I would be introduced to a number of guide dog puppies who were in the late stages of training so Becca and the team could get a better idea of exactly what kind of dog might be a good fit for me. Part of their remit was to match owners and dogs, like old-fashioned marriage brokers. Between them, Becca and her fellow London-based instructors had an encyclopaedic knowledge of the personalities and capabilities of all the guide dogs that were about to finish their training and also of the prospective owners and their lifestyles.

Seema came with me to the hotel on the Euston Road where I would be staying on my own overnight. Once we'd checked in, she described the layout of my room to me and then helped me find the way from the hotel to the Guide Dogs offices nearby, where I would be meeting the team at two o'clock sharp. Right on time, Becca appeared with the first dog – a young Labradoodle called Velda.

After Velda and I had been introduced, Velda was put into harness and we set off for a short walk around the area with Becca. It was my first time walking with an actual guide dog and I have to admit I was nervous. When Becca was on the other end of the harness, I knew I was safe. How would it be with a real animal? Would I be able to control it? Becca chose a quiet route, of course, but even so I quickly encountered some of the problems that face guide dog owners every day. People distracted by their phones walked straight into me. Others tried to distract the dog, despite the fact that she was obviously working.

Fortunately, Velda was a laid-back sort of canine so she didn't drag me along like a runaway horse as I'd feared she might. On the contrary, Velda was very slow and had to be coaxed to keep up with me. I did my best to encourage her, praising her all the way, but it didn't take long before Becca and I realized it was no good. For me, walking with Velda was like dancing with someone with two left feet.

A second dog, Suzie, a black Labrador, was an equally bad match for me. I was beginning to understand that, compared to the average VIP, I walk fast. Like Velda, Suzie preferred a slower pace. I felt as though I was going to trip over her all the time as she ambled along the pavement without any sense of urgency at all. I started to wonder if all the dogs were like this. Before I'd lost my sight, I'd seen dogs haring around the park fast as lightning. Was there something about being in harness that slowed them down? Would I have to adjust my pace permanently to accommodate a canine guide?

'Let's try one more,' said Becca.

The third dog, Beau, was a black Labrador. Like the other

two pups, Beau was going through his advanced training. I said hello, then Becca put Beau into harness and we set off again. Thankfully this experience was better. A lot better, in fact. Unlike the other two dogs, Beau easily matched my pace. He was a strong, confident pup and this quickly rubbed off on me. I liked him immediately and he seemed to like me back. I could imagine working with him. He responded at once to the commands I gave him. I was relieved he seemed to know his left from his right! I quickly came to understand that, like people, all dogs have different personalities and also walk at different paces. Beau and I walked together for an hour that day and I loved every minute of it. Could he be the one for me? I hoped so.

Seema joined me at the hotel again that evening for dinner. She met Beau and, as I had done, she fell in love with him at once. He was a really happy dog, who seemed pleased to be in our company. While we ate, he sat under the table, with his head on my feet – a very trusting gesture. We would have been happy to take him home but, alas, over dinner we learned that Beau had already been matched. He'd just been brought along to see how I got along with a dog of his temperament and style.

Though he was promised elsewhere, Beau was allowed to stay with me in my room overnight. At dinner, Becca had given us a crash course in how to keep the dog under control when away from her expert guidance. She told us what to do if the dog tried to get on the bed. Things like that. Fortunately, Beau's behaviour was exemplary. I slept like a log. Walking with guide dogs for the first time, and the excitement of thinking that one of them might be *my* guide dog, had taken it out of me.

I was sorry that Beau wasn't going to be mine, but meeting him had given me the confidence to believe that there was another dog out there that would be perfect for me. Likewise, the experience of walking with a dog in harness – albeit under heavy supervision – had convinced me that it was something I could get used to. The following morning I told Becca that I was very happy to continue the search for a match.

In July 2015, Becca called to let me know I'd officially been put on Guide Dogs' waiting list. The list had three tiers, she explained. Top priority for new matches went to current guide dog owners whose dogs were coming up for retirement. Guide dogs usually retire at the age of ten or eleven, she explained, and it is important to try to make the changeover seamless. The second tier was for those who have been on Guide Dogs' waiting list for more than six months. And the third tier was for new additions to the waiting list, like me.

Because I was relatively low priority, I was warned that I could be looking at a two-and-a-half-year wait. All the same, Becca asked me what my preferences were regarding breed and colour. With the caveat that I would prefer not to have a German shepherd because of Seema's childhood experience, I still didn't know enough about dogs to have a view on breed, so I let Becca choose for me. Likewise, Seema and I didn't have any issues with allergies and I wasn't fussy about dog hair like those City types! Now that I'd been through the assessment process, I was just keen to be matched with a dog as soon as possible. I didn't care whether that dog was black, blond or electric blue with pink stripes, so long as it could keep up with me.

Once I'd been put on the list, I tried not to think too much about it. I couldn't throw away my white cane just yet. Two and a half years was a long time. It could take even longer than that. I knew I had to keep living my life as though I might never get a dog. So it was a big surprise when only six weeks later Becca called again. I remember it clearly. It was four in the afternoon on a Tuesday.

'Amit, are you sitting down?' she asked. 'We think we've found a match for you.'

'Already?'

'Yes. But she's a bit of a tricky dog. She might like you, she might not.'

'Let's hope she likes me!' I said.

Becca laughed. She told me all about the newly qualified pup. She was a yellow Labrador, just turned eighteen months old. She had a big personality and was highly intelligent. She had also been quite a handful in training. Becca finished the description by telling me, 'Her name is Kika.'

While going through the assessment process, I'd learned that the puppies in each new guide dog litter are given names beginning with the same letter. So there is a 'C' litter, a 'D' litter and an 'F' litter, etc. Seema found this naming protocol very amusing. It's considered bad form to change a guide dog's name once it's finished its training, not least because it is so key to the training process, so there was every chance I might end up with a dog whose name I found embarrassing to shout in the park. Seema thought that was hilarious and entertained herself by coming up with the worst puppy names she could think of. But when I told her that I'd been matched with a dog called Kika, she was momentarily lost for words.

'Shut up!' she said. 'You're joking.'

'Why would I joke about that? She's called Kika. What's so funny?'

'Amit, you do know that Kika is my mum's maiden name?'

Until that moment, it had slipped my mind that Seema's mum was a Kika too.

When we told my parents, they were very pleased, as were Seema's – though her mum was taken aback at the dog's name. I have a tendency to joke with and wind up my in-laws so she thought that I was teasing her, and it took a lot of convincing before she believed us. But from that moment on, the link made Kika even more special to us all. Everyone agreed she was meant to be a part of our family.

Still, Becca had warned me, 'Kika has her quirks.' She'd told me how hard it had been for Kika to bond with her puppy walkers and her trainers, and if she failed to bond with me then it wouldn't be the right fit for either of us. Kika was a Marmite dog. She either loved or hated new people. And I was going to find out which category I fell into when Becca brought Kika to meet me the following Thursday.

For the next few days, I could barely sleep. I was so nervous, anxious and excited. Sometimes I felt like a child waiting for his birthday. At other times I felt like I was waiting for the results of a horrible exam I was certain I'd failed. It helped a little that some of Seema's cousins from Canada were spending most of the week with us.

Having some time to bond with the family was great and also very important. Seema's cousins, like most of the extended family, didn't really know the detail of what had happened and how much we'd gone through. They were clearly worried about how we were both coping. This was my first opportunity to really discuss what had happened in person. Talking about my progress and everything that I'd been doing reassured them and in return I got some much-needed support and a pep talk!

Seema's cousins kept me busy and distracted – we did all the big touristy things in London, entertained the children and had lots of giggles – but the fact that in a very short time I was going to meet Kika was always at the back of my mind.

As the day of my first meeting with Kika drew closer, I prepared the flat with the same care as you might for a visit from the Queen. I must have vacuumed a hundred times.

I've always been house-proud. Now, because I can't see it, I'm constantly paranoid that the house is dirty so I vacuum far more than I need to. My home is my sanctuary and I know every corner of it, even if I don't know how it looks exactly. I know my way around and know where things are. In the flat (as is the case in the home where we live now) we didn't have a coffee table in the middle of the living room as it would have been a trip hazard for me. Instead, I had an open space with only a few large pieces of furniture around the sides that were easy to keep clean.

People are always surprised when they come over that our home looks 'normal' – perhaps because there are no visible modifications. I don't know what people are expecting – possibly handrails everywhere and no design or style? There are also photos all over the walls, which seems to astonish people. But even though I can't see them, I know the memories that they represent and it is a comfort to have them around.

While I made sure the flat was immaculate, Seema bought cake to offer Kika's handlers. If we had to bribe the Guide Dogs team to let us have this dog, we would.

The big day arrived. Right on time, Becca rang the doorbell. She had brought Roz Wakelin with her. And Roz had brought Kika. I buzzed our visitors in and stood at the front door to our flat waiting to hear them walk up the corridor. When I heard the pitter-patter of Kika's four paws my heart started pounding in time. Would she like us? Would we like her? Was this going to be the start of something wonderful or a great big disappointment? I could hardly stand the suspense.

I welcomed Roz, Becca and Kika into the flat. Once they were inside, Roz let Kika off the lead. Completely ignoring Seema and me, as though we were mere hotel staff, Kika walked straight into the main bedroom.

'She's going to have a bit of a nose,' Roz explained. 'I hope you don't mind.'

How could we? If Kika was going to be part of the family, she needed to like where she'd be living.

Having checked out the bedroom, Kika explored the kitchen, the bathroom and the spare room. She walked from room to room, as though she was an estate agent evaluating the flat for a sale, with a slightly paranoid Seema right behind her. Meanwhile, we waited nervously to discover Kika's opinion. Paws up or paws down? Eventually, once she'd checked out every corner, Kika joined us in the living room. She found a sunny spot on the rug and sat down with a happy sigh. At least I hoped it was a happy sigh!

'She's OK,' Roz reassured me.

I had yet to give Kika so much as a pat. I didn't want to be pushy. I'd decided before she arrived that the best way to proceed was to let her set the pace. All the same, it was agony waiting for Kika to make her mind up as to whether she wanted to get to know me better. It was a long ten minutes before Kika deigned to come over to me for a tickle behind the ears. My relief when she did so was enormous.

'She likes you,' Roz confirmed.

After a cup of tea and some of the emergency bribery cake, Becca and Roz told me that it was time for the real test. We were going for a walk. Roz had Kika put on her harness – she didn't refuse and throw herself on the floor this time, thank goodness – and we set off on one of the routes I'd practised with Stella.

The first walk Kika and I took together was along the docks to the local university campus. It was a reasonably challenging walk, during which Kika met with all sorts of new sights and sounds. She gamely ignored the belligerent Canada geese that lived on the dockside. And the noisy planes taking off and landing at nearby City Airport, drowning out any possibility of conversation as they passed right overhead, didn't seem to faze her either.

As we walked, I gave the commands I'd been taught by Becca and felt Kika respond through the harness. I'd been worried that she wouldn't listen to me but, as all good guide dogs are taught during their training, whoever holds the harness is the boss.

I was told that a guide dog needs a purpose for every outing – that's how they are trained – so we decided that we should walk to a bench. Unfortunately, after ten minutes, the heavens opened and Kika slowed her pace. Still, we had to get to the bench. We sat on the wet seat for a couple of seconds, then walked quickly back to the flat.

Back at home, Seema was anxiously waiting to find out how the walk had gone. I thought we'd done well but Becca and Roz were inscrutable in their responses. It felt like another lifetime went by before Becca said, 'Amit, I'll see you in ten days,' and we knew that Kika and I had passed the first test – Becca had decided we were compatible. We were going to start proper training. I was going to be a guide dog owner at last.

13

Taking the Lead

Ten days later, I was on my way to Redbridge, where Kika and I would be staying with the Guide Dogs team for ten nights in a hotel near the training centre, as we learned how to work together on a core skills training course.

Seema was going to New York on business that week. It wasn't ideal timing since it would be the first time I'd spent more than a single night away from her since losing my sight. The time difference, Seema's work and the training I was about to embark on really amplified the feeling of being a long way from each other, and the idea of the next few weeks was very stressful for us both.

Luckily my parents stepped in to drive me to the hotel. We arrived early and Mum and Dad helped me get familiar with the layout of the huge room that would be my home for the next couple of weeks. The guide dogs were not due to arrive until 4.30 p.m. My parents were very excited to meet the newest member of Team Patel and waited for as long as they could to see her. They were only able to spend five minutes with her before they had to leave, but she graciously allowed them to pet her.

I soon discovered Kika had come to the hotel with more luggage than I had. Becca helped me to set up Kika's bed in my room and unpacked the things she would need for the course. Her water and food bowls, her grooming kit, her toys – all the things that would make Kika feel relaxed in this environment that was as strange to her as it was to me.

After that, we went back down to the lobby to meet the people and dogs taking the course alongside us. There were two other VIPs getting new dogs that day, both women. One was on her second, replacing her beloved first dog who was ready to retire. The other, like me, was getting her very first dog. By coincidence, she'd been paired with Suzie, with whom I'd taken a test walk on the Euston Road. I was glad to see that Suzie had found her perfect match. In another happy coincidence, I also discovered that Kika was actually sister to Beau, the black Labrador I'd met that same day. Then it all made sense, why I felt so comfortable with Kika's pace and style – she was strong and confident like her brother and that filled me with confidence too. Beau didn't have a name beginning with K despite being from a K litter because he was a sponsored dog and his sponsors had chosen to call him something different.

There was to be no official training on our first day at the hotel, so Becca sent us back to our rooms to rest with our dogs until she collected us all for dinner.

There was a festive atmosphere in the hotel restaurant that night. We were all so happy to be there, with our new dogs sitting quietly beneath the table. We shared stories about how we had come this far and how pleased we were to have been matched with our guide dogs at last. Both my new friends had been waiting over a year for their dogs; it felt like the beginning of a real adventure for all of us.

After dinner, it was time for one last toilet stop for the dogs before bedtime. Becca had set up a special pen where they could do their business – 'spend', as it's called in guide dog parlance. For now, Becca would be doing all the pooper scooping. Lucky Becca.

Once the dogs' comfort had been attended to, we all went back to our respective rooms. As I walked back to my room with Kika in harness, I was still nervous and excited about what the next ten days had in store for me. First things first, I FaceTimed Seema in New York so that I could tell her how things were going so far and, more importantly, so that she could see Kika. She told me she'd been on tenterhooks all day, eager to hear that Kika was as lovely as she remembered. I reassured her that Kika was just perfect. After that, I sat on the floor with Kika for a little while, getting to know her better. After we'd met Kika for the first time at our flat, Seema had described her for me: 'Her fur is white-blonde and she has soulful brown eyes and a lovely pink nose. It looks as though she's caught the sun.'

I chatted to Kika, telling her how honoured I felt to have been matched with such a magnificent pup, and she seemed happy to be around me, letting me scratch behind her ears and rub her belly. When at last she got up and took herself to bed, I did the same.

After a day of travel and the excitement of getting to meet Kika again, I was very tired and I quickly fell asleep. However, I hadn't been out for long when I was woken by the unfamiliar sound of scratching. It took a moment or two before I remembered that I wasn't at home and I wasn't sharing my room with Seema; I was in the hotel in Redbridge for the training camp. The scratching sound must be coming from Kika. I sat up and listened hard. Was there a problem? Was she trying to get out? To escape?

I got myself out of bed and checked the door to the corridor. It was firmly shut. I could find no obvious problem. Then I felt my way across the unfamiliar room, over to Kika's bed. When I crouched down next to her, to my surprise, she seemed to be fast asleep.

'Kika?' I said, questioningly.

She seemed to be asleep – she certainly ignored me – but she was also sitting up and seemed to be digging. I realized then something that nobody had told me – or rather *warned* me – about: dogs have dreams too. Kika was doing the canine equivalent of talking in her sleep. Perhaps the new environment had unsettled her and that was why she was dreaming particularly energetically that night.

At last, sensing that I was nearby, she woke up. She pressed her head against me as I sat down by her bed and talked to her for a few minutes to reassure her. Perhaps it was more to reassure myself. Her soft fur beneath my fingers as she let me stroke her back to sleep was comforting.

'Sleep tight, Kika,' I said, as I climbed back into bed.

The morning after our arrival in Redbridge, our official training began. It was time to find out why Kika had her reputation for being a tough dog to crack.

True to the stories I'd heard from her trainer Roz, when I tried to put on Kika's harness by myself for the very first time, she did absolutely nothing to help me. On the contrary, she made it as difficult as possible, either by flinging herself onto the ground as Roz had described or by putting her head on the floor, while sticking her bum in the air in a yoga-style downward dog position. I could almost hear Kika laughing as I struggled to get her to stand up properly. She was testing me already. I couldn't believe it.

Fortunately, Becca wasn't having any of it. She spotted what was going on and came straight over. When she said 'Kika!' in her strict auntie voice, Kika immediately behaved herself. It was a useful early lesson in Kika's character. She was pushing the boundaries, working out what she could get away with now I was in charge. With Becca standing by, I got the harness on and experienced my first 'Kika shake'.

Training progressed with lots of treats and fuss. We started by walking with the dogs in harness along the wide, carpeted corridors of the hotel. To begin with, I had one hand on Kika's harness and kept the other one on the wall, to make sure that she didn't unbalance me until I was more used to her weight and strength. Later we weaved our way through obstacle courses made of traffic cones. I could hear that, compared to the other two dogs, Kika was quick to respond to commands. She didn't hesitate. At least she didn't hesitate when she felt like co-operating!

We practised recall that first day too. Recall is a very important command. The last thing you want is to let your guide dog off harness for playtime and have them refuse to come back.

The hotel had three floors but we didn't ever take the lift. Instead, we practised going up and down stairs, a common obstacle we would meet time and time again. After so long with a white cane, walking without it took some getting used to and I found relearning how to climb the stairs particularly hard. It was disconcerting to think that I might fall.

As predicted, I was reluctant to give up the control having a white cane had given me. Now that I could no longer feel my way forward, how would I know if there was a hazard on the pavement or even overhead? The blunt answer was that I wouldn't. As Becca reminded me, that was what Kika was for now. I wasn't entirely comfortable with putting so much trust in her, but I knew that unless I let Kika spot the obstacles for me, she would not be able to do her job. I had to learn to trust.

But how could I learn to trust a dog? Particularly one with Kika's reputation. By refusing to put her harness on, she'd already shown me that she had a wilful side. Her 'Kika shake' reminded me of a stroppy teen expressing her disdain at having to do something she'd rather not do. I imagined she'd been giving me the side eye all day too. I was way out of my comfort zone.

Again and again in those early days, I subconsciously held Kika back, not believing that her training could possibly have equipped her with the ability to do all the things I could with my white cane. No matter how often Becca assured me that Kika was doing just fine, I couldn't relax. Kika was just a dog, after all. And I am a control freak! I'd been so excited at the prospect of getting a guide dog, but now I was having doubts again. How was this going to work?

The third morning of our stay at the hotel was the game-changer. We had scheduled an early start as there was still a lot to get through before we could return home with our new dogs. When my alarm went off, I blearily trailed my hand along the bedroom wall to find the door to the en suite bathroom. However, when I got there, I found that Kika was blocking my way. She stood right in front of the door, solid as a piece of furniture, refusing to let me get by.

'Come on, Kika,' I said. 'I need to get in there.'

Still Kika wouldn't budge.

'Kika?' I tried again. 'Please? Get out of the way?'

Nope, Kika seemed to say as she marked my movements like a hockey player keeping another from the goal. I thought she was playing a game. I tried my best to persuade her with praise and pats, but I couldn't convince her to move – she continued to stand right in the middle of the doorway. I couldn't squeeze around her and I didn't want to step over her in case I tripped and fell.

'Kika?' I pleaded. I was tired. We were on a schedule. I needed her to get out of the way so I could get washed and dressed but, no matter how much I cajoled, Kika remained as immovable as a dog-shaped statue. Totally unable to shift her, I didn't know what to do. I sat back down on the bed and called Becca, who was on hand twenty-four seven for any emergencies.

I felt ridiculous as I told Becca the problem. 'It's Kika. She's blocking the bathroom door,' I said. 'She won't get out of the way. I've asked her nicely and I've tried raising my voice but she's not obeying any of my commands.'

'Really? That's not good. Lift her if you have to,' was Becca's response.

Lift her? I didn't imagine Kika would be too happy about that, but Becca reminded me I had to be confident in my commands and show that I meant business.

'You're the boss.'

When I put down the phone, I asked Kika to move again. Once again she refused.

'Kika.' I put a warning tone in my voice. Still no dice. So I took hold of her collar and physically hauled her out of the way, while simultaneously pushing open the bathroom door with my free hand.

As soon as I took one step into the bathroom, I realized that something was wrong. I could hear running water. The tiled floor was soaking wet and dangerously slippery. As I felt the water beneath my bare feet, I suddenly realized that Kika had been blocking my way because she knew there was a hazard on the other side of the door. She wasn't being difficult. Neither had she been mucking around. On the contrary, Kika had been looking out for me.

'Kika, I'm so sorry,' I said.

She didn't say 'I told you so' but she did accept a belly rub and a handful of treats in recompense.

The leak in the bathroom was a nuisance – it took the hotel management the best part of the day to sort it out – but in another way, that leak was very lucky, because it had given Kika the opportunity to show me what she was made of and prove to me that I could trust her – this dog who I'd known for a matter of days – with my life.

After that morning, everything was different. Now I knew for sure that Kika would do her best for me, I began to loosen up and let her take more control. I was no longer pulling her back all the time. Once I let her have free rein, Kika proved herself time and time again. I was humbled by her ability. How had I ever thought that a white cane was a better option than this amazing, intelligent and kindly creature who had, thank goodness, decided that she was going to let me welcome her into my life? I let her take the lead at last.

Over the next week, Becca took us out of the hotel onto the streets to practise the skills we'd learned in the hotel corridors in the real world. We did lots of kerb-to-kerb training. We walked around a shopping centre in nearby Ilford, to get used to walking through crowds. There were night walks too, so the dogs could practise working in different light conditions. We also attended lectures on caring for our new companions: how to groom them; how to make sure they were eating correctly (all those treats had to come out of a strict daily allowance); how to know when they needed to see a vet.

By the end of those ten days in Redbridge, Kika and I were a proper team. When Becca told me that she was satisfied with our progress and I could take Kika home, I could not stop grinning. It was September 2015. Just under two years since I lost my sight and now I had my guide dog. I felt like the luckiest man on earth.

14

Kika Comes Home

So though I'd been warned that Kika – the Marmite dog – might love me or hate me, we'd established a good rapport. We'd worked hard on the residential training course and seemed to be doing well together. But how would our bond work back in the real world? At home with Seema? On the commute? In all situations and all weathers? Day and night? Without Becca on hand to get us out of a fix?

Kika and I had learned to work together in the safe confines of a hotel, but I wanted to do more now and give back to the charities that had supported me. I had a plan to volunteer for the RNIB so I knew that my day-to-day would involve buses and trains and navigating busy London Tube stations at rush hour. How would Kika cope with all that?

Because I was not yet qualified as a guide dog owner, when Kika first came home with me, I wasn't actually allowed to take her out of the flat on my own. Becca warned me that it could be a further three months before that happened. In the meantime, Becca would come to the flat for two to three hours a day, six days a week, for what is known as 'development training', to help me and Kika learn and practise the routes that were essential to my daily life, such as going to the station or the supermarket. In order to qualify together,

Kika and I would need to show that we were working well as a team, that I was confident in my commands and she was obeying them, and that she was guiding me safely. Becca would be watching every step and be there to intervene in case we needed her.

People often ask me how Kika knows where we're going when we set off on a trip. It's quite simple: she doesn't. Kika, like all guide dogs, is trained to walk from kerb to kerb. At the beginning of the walk, I let her know where we're headed but I'll always direct her. It's up to me to know where we are and where we're going. If we get to a junction and I don't tell her otherwise, she'll continue on the route that is most familiar to her. For example, when I say that I want to go to the RNIB, Kika will take me to the train station. As we've already spent time learning the route, Kika knows that first she has to get off the train at London Bridge station. Somehow, at the station, Kika finds the barriers and if I don't steer her elsewhere, she knows the best route to get me to the Underground. The more routes we do together, the closer our bond and the more confident she is in where to go.

Most of the time, the train we need leaves from platform seven and I've got to know the people who work on that platform well over the years, but as anybody who has ever had to commute into London knows, platforms can be changed at a moment's notice. I have an app on my phone that helps with that, but sometimes it takes ages to find a signal, by which time the train I need might have already left the station. So what I usually do is ask Kika to find me a member of staff. Most of the time Kika does that with ease – she recognizes them by their high-vis jackets – though she has occasionally introduced me to random building contractors!

When we were training together, to get into the zone, Kika needed to be motivated. The team at Guide Dogs had long since worked out that she couldn't be in an office all day. She needed to be kept occupied with varied journeys. That's why she was a good match for me.

Kika was already used to the big city. With Becca, who was based out of Euston, she'd become acclimatized to central London. With Roz, she had even visited Westminster (though not gone into any buildings) as part of her training in the city environment. She was used to crowds and busy pavements. In addition, Roz had trained Kika alongside a German shepherd, so Kika was not intimidated by other dogs, even big ones.

I had thought that home training with Becca would be a matter of teaching Kika my white cane routes, but I soon learned that wasn't the case. I had to be effectively retrained as well. With my white cane, I would occasionally take short-cuts, but Kika was trained to walk from kerb to kerb and to find crossings. I couldn't teach her bad habits if I wanted to be able to trust her in different situations later on. Once again, there was a lot to learn.

Ninety-nine per cent of guide dogs are trained to walk on the left of their VIP, because the tactile world is set up for the right-handed majority. Therefore, at crossings, Kika would duly place me on the right side, since that's where the unit with the button and the spinning cone to alert the visually impaired to when it's their turn to cross is. To ensure that Kika always drew me in that direction, Becca used bribes to catch her attention. A little mackerel pâté on the correct lamp post always worked.

Mackerel pâté came to the rescue again when it was time to teach Kika how to guide me in and out of the complex where Seema and I lived. Kika's natural instinct was to take me straight to the front of the gate, but since the control panel was off to the side, that wouldn't help me get in. Kika soon learned to follow the scent of mackerel to take me to the control panel first instead so that I could key in the code that opened the gate itself.

Mackerel pâté helped Kika to learn lots of new things, but when it came to escalator training, the bribes had to be bigger. Not all guide dogs are trained to use escalators. Those that are tend to be London-based dogs, whose owners need to be able to use the Tube, as I do. The dogs are assessed during their advanced training to see if they would be comfortable with such a challenge. Once a dog has undertaken escalator-training, it is considered 'qualified' and that status is marked in their official ID book. This entitles the dog to use escalators operated by Transport for London only. TfL's escalators have a particular configuration with long flat sections at the beginning and end that make it easy for a guide dog and owner to walk onto them. Escalators in other places, like department stores, usually end more abruptly.

One of the reasons why Becca had matched me with Kika was because she was escalator-trained. She'd learned with Roz while she was at Redbridge. Roz explained that she first got Kika used to the idea of a moving staircase on a flat travelator in a large supermarket near the training centre. The management there was very accommodating and used to seeing the guide dog puppies in store. They were happy to either stop or slow the travelator to help with the training too.

It was a great tool for getting Kika accustomed to the sound, the movement and to the feel of it on her paws. Sometimes, the very sensation of the metal slats puts a dog off. Fortunately, Kika didn't seem to mind it. The next stage was to entice her to step onto the travelator while it was moving. To do that, Roz had to bring out some serious treats.

Led by her nose from the start, Kika always hung out for the smelliest titbits imaginable. It was as though she'd learned that if she seemed to be hesitating, her trainers would have to bring out something better as a reward. Roz told me that once, in desperation, she resorted to using hot chicken wings from the supermarket's rotisserie to entice Kika to step onto the travelator. With many more treats of that calibre, Kika slowly graduated from the flat moving belt to a proper moving staircase. Roz trained Kika to stand still on the escalator until it started to level out, at which point she could safely hop off.

Soon Kika was happy enough to go up an escalator but, like many dogs, she hated travelling down one as she couldn't see where she was going as easily. More rotisserie chicken wings got her over her hesitation.

Kika and I took the escalator together for the first time about two weeks after she came to live with me. It was at our nearest Tube station, Canning Town, on the Jubilee Line. It was a big moment for both of us and I was nervous. I'd long since mastered the art of using an escalator with my white cane. I would seek out the handrail and take my time stepping on. With Kika, I was worried she would drag me onto the escalator before I was ready.

Becca reassured me as she explained the protocol: Kika would not step onto the escalator until I told her to. She would always take the lead from me. I took a deep breath and gave the command – 'forward'. Going up, Kika was fine. She got on and found the correct position right away, standing by my side with her front paws on the step ahead. Going down, she hesitated. For a moment it was hairy but we managed it. As we successfully completed the manoeuvre for the first time, I would have given Kika all the chicken wings in the world.

These days, Kika has no problem with escalators at all and she absolutely loves travelators whenever we come across them. However, like me, Kika's not for standing still on one. She likes to walk along them, enjoying the sense of speed that gets her ears flapping. Also like me, she gets frustrated with trolleys. I can feel her head bobbing from side to side as she looks for a way to get by them. She can't stand dawdlers! As Kika's got older, she's definitely developed something of a London attitude towards slow walking. If people won't get out of her way, they better expect to be muscled aside.

Just a couple of weeks into development training, there came a day when neither Becca nor Roz was able to come with me on a walk. I thought that Kika and I were facing a day confined to the house, but Becca said that Kika and I were allowed to go out with Seema.

We jumped at the chance, deciding to go to Canary Wharf, which was where Seema was working at the time. We headed for the train station. Kika walked on my left, as she has been trained to do, with me holding her lead and her harness handle. On the train platform, Kika waited patiently for the train to stop and for me to issue the command to find the doors. On boarding, at another command, she found me somewhere to sit, indicating an empty space by placing her head on a seat. I followed her head down with my (free) right hand. If there's no seat available, or no one gets up for us, then Kika will find a space within the carriage for us to stand, before sitting by my feet or even laying down if there's enough space.

On this first train journey with Seema, Kika behaved in exemplary style, which reassured Seema that when Kika and I were licensed to head out alone, Kika would look after me. When we arrived at the station, we found that a crowd had gathered on the plaza. The Rugby World Cup was in full swing and the legendary New Zealand team, the All Blacks, were meeting their fans.

Before I lost my sight, I was a big rugby fan, so Seema and I stopped to listen to the All Blacks talking to the crowd. When one of the players spotted me with Kika, we were invited up onto the stage and Kika was appointed the team's unofficial mascot for the tour. She posed for pictures like a true professional. Though they aren't my team, I'm pleased to say that the All Blacks won the tournament that year. Kika obviously worked her magic.

Only a week after that magical encounter – and far sooner than Becca had estimated – she decided that Kika and I were ready to take on the world alone. It was the best news. At last I was qualified to own a guide dog. I was given a contract setting out my obligations to Kika, such as looking out for her health and her happiness, and handed over a fifty pence piece in symbolic payment, making it legally binding. From that moment on, Kika and I were officially licensed to go anywhere together. It was like passing my driving test and ripping up the learner plates. I was ecstatic.

On our first official solo outing together, Kika and I went to meet Seema off the DLR when she came home from work. Stepping out with Kika was a completely different experience to walking with my white cane. There was no bumping into bins, lamp posts, letterboxes, no misjudging kerbs. Kika found the crossing first time and took me straight to the button. She then took me straight to the stairs at the DLR without my having to fumble around and walked me safely up them to the platform.

The relief that came with letting Kika take me to my destination was immense. There is so much mental pressure that comes with using a white cane. I was always switched on, on high alert, and the smallest of journeys would leave me both physically and psychologically exhausted. With Kika, once I learned to trust her, that load was lifted and eventually I would find I had more energy to channel into different things.

But for now, I was just happy to be able to get around again. Seema was over the moon to see us both standing there when she stepped off the train. It was a very proud moment indeed.

Kika and I now began to really get to know each other. The more time I spent with her, the more I came to understand her personality. Though she had been expertly trained to do things in the best and proper guide dog fashion, she would often do what she thought she could get away with instead. Kika was as fond of a shortcut as I was! Whereas before she would walk from kerb to kerb, now on a familiar route she would follow the side of a building round instead. In our first few weeks together, I sensed that she was trying to work out how much I could see. In order to make sure that Kika worked to her best ability, I was instructed never to tell her where to go, even if I thought I might be walking into a lamp post. In this way, Kika came to learn how much she needed to navigate.

Though thankfully Kika didn't ever walk me into a lamp post, I soon discovered that inanimate objects were the least of the hazards we'd encounter. People don't always get out of the way for us. This can be especially scary on train platforms where someone not moving out of the way forces us to walk closer to the edge of the platform. People also shoulder-barge me as they pass by, shoulders tensed on purpose, because Kika and I have the audacity to walk in a straight line and not move out of the way for them. Some people even walk straight at us, like it's a game of chicken, to see whether I or Kika will react and move. Often they move out of the way at the very last minute, resulting in bumping into us or us being hit by bags. It's very frustrating.

As well as her tendency to cut corners, Kika's love of food was an issue at first. Seema and I spent a lot of time working on Kika's ability to ignore stuff dropped on the street. To do that Seema would go out ahead of us on walks, laying temptation along the route. People must have thought she was nuts, putting down bits of chicken on the pavement. But there was method in the madness. As Kika and I came along afterwards,

Seema would be able to tell me where the traps were laid so that when Kika successfully ignored one, I could praise her. However, it didn't always work, as Kika could be sneaky.

Once, when we'd just started a walk, I suspected that Kika had picked something up. But Seema couldn't see anything in Kika's mouth – in fact, her mouth wasn't even moving – and when Seema asked Kika to drop what she was carrying, Kika looked at her with a 'butter wouldn't melt' expression that persuaded Seema she was mistaken. We carried on for some time, but I was still convinced Kika had something as her walk seemed a bit odd, as if she was distracted. We stopped again a few minutes later, except this time, I opened up her mouth – not easily I might add. It was almost as if she had something to hide – and that was when a whole stale doughnut fell out! While Kika might be a highly trained guide dog, she is still a food-obsessed Labrador after all, albeit a very clever one!

I also learned that Kika was a moody girl. Seema has only recently told me that Kika never smiled her doggy smile for the first six months she was with us unless she was being chased around a park. These days, Kika smiles all the time. Unless she has to work late, that is. Then she puts on her 'bitchy resting face' and makes her displeasure felt with the 'Kika shake' that asks, 'Why are we still out?' She knows she won't get fed until we're home.

She also hates to get wet, despite her love of dirty water as a puppy. Ordinarily, Kika does her best to guide me around every puddle, as she's been trained to do. If she has to walk in the rain, however, she walks round the puddles herself but is more than happy to drag me right through them in her haste to be back home in the warm and dry.

She's nosy too. When we're walking through the city, her concentration is epic. In an environment like busy Bank station, she's on a mission, increasing her pace to keep up with the crowds, sticking close to the wall and taking me through abrupt ninety-degree turns to get where we need to be. On a more leisurely walk, especially if it's a route she knows well, I can feel her head swinging from side to side as she checks out what's happening in the neighbourhood. She peers through every open gate. Fortunately, while Kika's always keen to see what's going on, she doesn't allow herself to be too distracted. If she sees a squirrel, for example, she won't chase it. Likewise she ignores cats and other dogs. If she's on the harness, she won't even greet any other dogs apart from one in particular – an old male terrier – that she seems to have a special fondness for. I hear her making happy noises whenever he comes into view.

Ultimately, when Kika's on the harness she's on duty. Off the harness, she's a typical Labrador, searching out people who'll give her a fuss. Actually, she'll sometimes do that when she's strictly on duty too. If we're on the train and I'm safely sitting down, Kika will stare at neighbouring passengers with her big brown eyes until they come over and say hello. On the flip side, if she doesn't like someone, she'll make that known too. When we're out and about, she'll cross the street to avoid anyone she doesn't like the look of. It wasn't obvious in the early days. I always assumed Kika was crossing the street to avoid obstacles. It was only when I was out with Seema that she was able to tell me what Kika was really doing. Now I've learned the tell-tale signs – Kika will suddenly get a burst of energy while walking as she diverts to a kerb. It's not just strangers – on a number of occasions we've visited friends only to find that while Kika likes the children, she's not keen on their parents. When that happens, unfortunately Kika doesn't bother with social niceties. If she wants to be elsewhere, she positions herself by the front door and harrumphs and stares until I tell her it's time to go home.

Kika's tendency to take strong views about the people she meets was a bit of a problem when I first brought her back to our flat. While Kika was becoming well bonded with me, for some reason she decided that she didn't like Seema at all.

Kika made her feelings very clear. On several occasions, when Seema walked into a room, Kika walked out. Sometimes she would physically barge Seema out of the way in her haste to get past her. When we were relaxing in the living room, Seema and I would often sit on the floor together so that Kika wouldn't feel left out, since she wasn't allowed on the sofa. When we did that, Kika would squeeze her way between us and turn round and round in a tight circle until we were forced to make more space for her. Then she would plonk herself down with a deep sigh and rest her head on my lap, ignoring Seema completely.

No matter how hard Seema tried to connect with her, no matter how many treats she bribed her with, Kika simply did not want to know. We were desperate to understand why Kika was behaving so strangely and how on earth we could change the situation. Was she jealous of Seema? If that was the case, then we had a problem on our hands. I didn't want to have to choose between Kika and my wife!

When we thought and talked more about it, it started to become a little clearer. In her short life, Kika had experienced a lot of change. She'd lived with two sets of puppy walkers, then she'd spent time at the Guide Dogs kennel and now she was in a different place again with us. We already knew that Kika had taken a while to bond with her trainer Roz. Had Kika developed abandonment issues during her puppy-walking days, which led her to distrust that the new people she met were going to stick around? Had we inadvertently played into Kika's fears? I'd brought Kika home for the first time on a Friday. The very next day, Seema had gone out to a friend's baby shower. With Seema out at work almost every weekday, did Kika think that Seema wasn't worth getting to know and love because she wasn't always around?

We could only hope that more time, more treats and growing familiarity would solve the problem. In the mean-time, poor Seema did her best not to be too put out that the new female in my life seemed to want me all to herself.

15

A Brush with the Law

In October 2015, only a few weeks after I qualified to take Kika out unsupervised, Seema and I were due to go to Amsterdam to celebrate her father's sixtieth birthday along with all of her family. The trip had been booked for months and was supposed to be a surprise for her father. Since Kika had only recently come into our lives, and it had all come about so quickly, I knew I would have to pull out. Kika and I were still getting used to one another and, in accordance with Guide Dogs' guidelines, it would be another six months before we were allowed to travel abroad together, to make sure we were properly bonded. So while Seema joined the rest of the Mistry clan in the Netherlands, I would have to stay behind.

I was sad to be missing what was bound to be a great party, but I was pretty confident that Kika and I would be OK on our own for the weekend. I'd got used to being alone in the flat long before she came along. That was no problem. And it would be a quiet weekend; I didn't have anywhere in particular I needed to be. Seema had stocked up the fridge for us and we had our well-practised walks for when Kika needed exercise. The rest of the time, we would relax and enjoy ourselves and continue to get to know each other better.

I reassured Seema that everything would be fine in her absence. I wanted her to enjoy her dad's birthday to the full.

Seema left for Amsterdam on a Friday. On the first night, Kika and I hung out in the flat together. I could tell that Kika enjoyed having my full attention without having to compete with my wife! Meanwhile, I enjoyed having someone to chat to, even if Kika only gave the occasional loud yawn in response.

On Saturday afternoon, it was time to take Kika out for some exercise. The weather was changeable but I decided we had time to take a walk along the docks to the university between rain showers. It was the route we'd taken on our very first walk together.

Kika knew the university walk well by now and it all went swimmingly until we got to the university gate. It was closed. I asked the security guard for help but he wouldn't let us through. This meant we couldn't do our usual circuit. The guard told me that we would have to walk right around the campus instead.

Realizing that the guard would not be moved, I took a deep breath and worked out what to do next. Thus far, Kika and I had always stuck to routes we knew well, but I figured that it was as good a time as any for us to experiment with finding a new route spontaneously. This sort of thing was bound to happen eventually.

'Forward.'

I gave Kika her instructions and we set off in what I thought was the right direction to get back to the flat. I estimated that we were almost halfway back home when Kika suddenly stopped. She sat down, right on my feet, which I knew meant she was serious about wanting me to stop too. I had no idea what had spooked her and why she being was so insistent.

'Kika?'

I asked her to get up and keep going. She refused. Instead she continued to sit on my feet, with all her puppy weight.

'Forward, Kika,' I tried again.

Nope. She was not going anywhere. Kika was as immovable as she had been on the morning when she kept me out of the wet bathroom. All the same, I was more irritated than trusting when she refused my commands this time. Of all the moments for her to decide she wasn't going to walk . . . The weather was starting to take a turn for the worse. It was getting cold. It was windy. It felt like it was going to rain. I just wanted to get back to the flat.

'Forward, Kika.' I tried using a more authoritative tone. Still she would not move.

'Kika?' A softer tone didn't work either.

'Kika!' She definitely didn't respond to frustration.

'Ki-kaaa . . .' Or pleading.

She simply stood – or rather sat – her ground.

As far as I could tell, there was no one nearby to ask for help. The only thing I could think of to do was call Guide Dogs' support team and ask them what on earth I was supposed to do now.

A member of the support team answered the phone at once but there was nothing they could do for me. Everything they suggested, I had already tried. I couldn't even really tell them where I was. There was no handy Burger King stinking nearby.

In desperation, I called the police.

You can imagine how stupid I felt as I explained my dilemma to the operator who answered my 999 call.

'What's your emergency?' the operator asked.

'I'm blind and I've got a guide dog but she's refusing to move.'

I expected the operator to think I was a prankster. Guide dogs do as they're told, right? That's the whole point. Fortunately, I was connected to a sympathetic operator who was a big dog lover and she believed me when I explained that I thought Kika was stopping for a reason. I told the operator where I thought I was. She told me to stay calm and promised to send help at once.

It was only a few minutes later that a police car arrived. They'd received the call to look out for me just as they were driving by. The officers got out of their car to assist me. I was embarrassed to need their help and started to apologize on Kika's behalf but they cut me short. They told me that as soon as they saw me they'd understood why Kika had taken a stand – or a sit.

'Don't worry about it. She did the right thing,' one of the officers said at once.

It turned out that I had inadvertently chosen a route home that was taking us between a dual carriageway and a building site. The pavement was in the process of being dug up. There were cones all over the place. The wind had blown some of those cones onto the path we'd previously walked, making it difficult to navigate. We were effectively penned in. The only way through was by walking out into the busy road and Kika, understandably, didn't want to do that. She'd been protecting me again.

'She knows what she's doing,' the other officer said admiringly. 'Clever girl.'

Rather than let us walk on, the police officers suggested they give Kika and me a lift home. Cold and tired after being out for much longer than I'd intended, I readily agreed to their offer. Kika was only too happy to jump into the police car and rest her paws.

As we were being driven back home, I called Seema.

'You'll never guess where I'm calling you from . . .' I said.

'A police car! I leave you alone for one day!' said Seema when she heard the story. 'One day! Honestly, Amit. What am I going to do with you both?'

As Seema laughed at my retelling of the whole scenario, it started to seem funnier to me too, especially when I imagined what the security guards at home would think when I rocked up in the back of a squad car. As predicted, they thought it was hilarious.

Back at the flat, I called Guide Dogs to let them know how the situation had unfolded. They weren't surprised to hear what Kika had done. Kika had practised avoiding kerb obstructions at the training centre in Redbridge but, of course, her training was of no use when she was faced with kerb obstructions *and* a busy road that left her no way of safely getting through. In the event, Kika had made the right decision. Once again, she'd proved that she knew what she was doing and she would never, ever willingly endanger my life.

When Seema came home from Amsterdam, we continued to do our best to improve her relationship with Kika. Seema had adored Kika from the get-go, but Kika remained cautious, snubbing Seema even more because she'd been away for a few days again. Kika's bond and attachment was with me so she wanted to be by my side always, even if that meant physically pushing Seema out of the way to be next to me.

We'd told ourselves that Kika would not be allowed into the bedroom and set up her bed in the living room, but she wasn't having that and soon had us bending the rules. Perhaps sensing that Seema would be a pushover because she was trying to build their relationship, Kika tested the boundaries. In the middle of the night, she would leave her bed, come into our room and sleep on the floor if she had to. She just wanted to be nearby. Eventually, we gave up on trying to keep her out of the bedroom.

Sometimes, life with Kika was like living with an overgrown furry toddler, determined to rule the house. But regardless of her quirks, we were falling deeply in love with her.

16

Channelling My Energy

November quickly rolled around and with it came Kika's first Diwali.

Diwali – the Hindu festival of light – has always been a big deal for me. As a child, it was the highlight of my year. There was a wonderful two-week build-up of preparations for the big day when the entire extended family would meet at the temple before heading home for a huge feast. However, when I lost my sight, I lost my religion too. I stopped going to the temple. I stopped meditating. I felt like there was no point. Seema and my parents knew better than to try to persuade me otherwise. But in the short time I'd known Kika, she'd filled me with a confidence and optimism I'd thought I'd lost forever. She made me want to celebrate life again. She made me believe there was something bigger out there, looking out for me. I couldn't wait to take her to the temple for the most important festival in the Hindu calendar. With Kika, I could hold my head up high.

That year Seema and I planned to go with my parents, my brother Mital and his wife Kirsty to the temple in Neasden – the BAPS Shri Swaminarayan Mandir – which is the biggest Hindu temple outside India.

I'd been to the Neasden Temple many times before I lost

my sight – the last time was Diwali 2013 – so I remembered well how spectacular it is. It's constructed from Bulgarian limestone and Italian marble, which was all sent to India to be carved by traditional artisans. Once the carving was done, the 26,000 individually numbered stone pieces were shipped back to London where the building was assembled like a giant three-dimensional jigsaw. The temple has seven gold-tipped pinnacles and five domes. Beneath the seven pinnacles are seven shrines. Every surface is covered with the most intricate decoration. At Diwali, the shrines are festooned with flowers and sweets and huge dishes of vegetarian food for the ceremony of Annakut, when we offer our gratitude to the Hindu god Krishna. It's a real feast for the eyes and the smells are delicious too.

I couldn't wait but, as Diwali crept closer, Seema admitted that she wasn't entirely sure it was a great idea to take Kika with us. She reminded me that the temple would be incredibly busy and loud with the festivities. Mital too had his doubts. He went one further. He told me he had taken the initiative and called the temple and had been told that dogs were not allowed. Kika would *have* to stay home.

I wasn't having that. No way. Thanks to the RNIB, I was well versed in access issues and the rights of people with assistance animals. Brushing Seema and Mital's concerns aside, I called the temple myself and the person I spoke to agreed that there should be no problem with my taking Kika to the temple, which was a public place. It wasn't as though there were never any dogs at the temple, after all. At busy times, the security team sometimes used sniffer dogs to speed up their checks. A guide dog would surely be welcome.

So we travelled to Neasden to celebrate Diwali as planned. I was certain that there wouldn't be an issue.

Men and women are segregated inside this particular temple, so while Seema went in with Mum and my sister-in-law Kirsty, I followed Dad and my brother to join the other men. However, when we got to the front of the queue, I was told that I would have to leave Kika outside.

'Dogs aren't allowed.'

'But Kika is an assistance animal.' I then confidently reminded the security guard of my rights.

Still he refused to let Kika come into the temple. He suggested instead that I tie Kika to a railing outside the building and pick her up again on the way out.

'There's no way I'm going to do that,' I told him.

Apart from the fact that Kika would not be happy left outside on her own, her training had cost tens of thousands of pounds. She wasn't just a much-loved member of my family, she was an incredibly valuable working animal and I had promised to look after her and signed a contract to that effect. So I stood my ground. The security guard stood his. I felt my frustration turning into anger.

In the end, another security guard came up with a workable compromise.

'Please leave your dog with me,' he said. 'I've got Labradors at home. I'll take care of her.'

By this time I was ready to abandon the temple visit altogether but I knew Dad and Mital would be disappointed. So Kika remained with the animal-loving security guard while the three of us went on inside. Having kept us standing around for so long, the head of security offered to guide us around so that we could skip the queues and get back to Kika as quickly as possible. Inside the temple, Dad acted as my guide, while I carried Kika's harness on my shoulder. Some bright spark asked which one of us was the dog. It didn't help my mood.

I got to visit the shrines and make my offerings but the whole episode had left a very bad taste in my mouth. I'd decided to go to the temple that day because having Kika made me feel like I could hold my head high again. Having to shuffle round hanging on to Dad was an entirely different experience from the one I'd planned. I felt like a second-class citizen. It was far from the joyful Diwali celebration I had hoped for.

Guide Dogs has always done its best to spread the word about access for the visually impaired but the fact was, as my experience in Neasden proved, there were some areas of the community that the message had yet to reach. The majority of the people working for Guide Dogs are white, as are the majority of guide dog owners. Churches have been admitting assistance animals for a long time, but temples and mosques were a different matter.

After my disappointing Diwali experience, I called the temple to discuss what had happened. When I explained that their failure to provide proper access was illegal, a temple representative simply said, 'We've never had a guide dog here before.'

Angry and upset at the lack of understanding I encountered, I tweeted about the situation. I'd joined Twitter as a sighted doctor, just to see what it was all about. As a new VIP, I used it to connect with other VIPs and ask questions about support and resources. This was the first time I'd tweeted in anger. It wasn't long before a journalist at the BBC picked the story up. I was invited onto BBC Asian Network radio to talk about accessing places of worship with an assistance animal alongside my now good friend Dave Kent from Guide Dogs. I got a great deal of support but some of the less sympathetic responses underlined the problem.

The fact is, many visually impaired Asians are reluctant to get guide dogs because, while the Hindu faith reveres all kinds of animals, disability still carries a stigma in many communities. Therefore, anything that draws attention to disability is a bad thing and a guide dog definitely draws attention to blindness.

The media attention meant that the Neasden Temple couldn't ignore the issue any longer. After speaking to me again, they came up with a compromise. They told me that while Kika wouldn't be allowed in the inner sanctum of the temple itself, out of concern for the other worshippers, they would make arrangements for her to be cared for in comfort and safety while I went inside. She would be allowed to stay in the office while I went around with a sighted guide. It wasn't perfect but it was a start. This was my chance to make any future visits for VIPs more comfortable than my own.

First things first, the temple needed some properly trained sighted guides. I swung into action to arrange for that training and, within a couple of weeks, I was back at the temple with Dave and a few more of his colleagues from Guide Dogs' London engagement team – Rob, Mel and Desi – and our dogs.

Both my parents and Seema had been trained in guiding

visually impaired people too. On one of the training days that my parents attended back when I was first matched to Kika, the Guide Dogs team blindfolded Mum with a 'mind fold' – a specially made mask to give her a sense of how I experienced the world. With the mind fold on, Mum realized the extent of what I had to deal with and she burst into tears. She'd had no idea how disorientating and isolating being deprived of one's sight can be. How frightening it is. I think it helped her understand how important Kika is to me.

There were plenty of volunteers for sighted guide training at the temple that day. We equipped them with mind folds such as the one Mum had worn, so that they too could experience the temple from my point of view. The volunteers were paired up, taking it in turns to either wear a mind fold or act as a guide. The guides were taught how to describe the terrain for their mind-folded partner, how to explain when they were approaching steps, slopes and corners, etc. They also learned how to approach a visually impaired person, how to offer assistance (for example, to offer their elbow) and how to walk safely side by side, even when passing through narrow spaces.

The volunteers soon discovered that the temple is a very difficult place to navigate without sight. The entrance is open plan with a shop and desks in the middle, but there are long corridors with slopes to walk down and stairs to climb before you can reach the temple itself. The inner sanctum is almost maze-like if you can't see, with marble pillars and cordons set up to mark out different zones. It's also full of disorientating echoes. To make things worse, at the time we trained our willing volunteers, there were no tactiles on the marble floors to guide a visually impaired person through. There were no proper handrails either.

That day, without the Diwali crowds to distract me, gave me an even clearer idea of the problems. All the same, I walked away from the training day thinking it had gone well. On the way out, the temple manager told me that I could call him directly whenever I wanted to visit. I took him up on his offer, and the next time I went to the temple a few months later, he guided me around himself, using the skills he'd learned with Guide Dogs, while Kika stayed in his office on her very own bed. (Yes, they'd bought a special bed for Kika by now.)

The Neasden Temple also took on board my concern that the very nature of the building made it a nightmare for the visually impaired. When the manager guided me around, I suggested that adding a few simple stick-on tactiles to handrails and the edges of stairs would be a good start. The RNIB could help them to find the right stuff to use. Just before the next Diwali, the manager called to tell me that he would like me to come and road-test the tactiles he'd had installed.

Given that the Neasden Temple is one of the most extravagantly beautiful places of worship in the world, I suppose I shouldn't have been surprised to discover that rather than disfigure the sumptuous marble interiors with nasty sticky dots, the temple committee had commissioned some brand new marble handrails, with the tactiles I'd suggested carved into the design. Realizing what an effort they had gone to in order to make the visually impaired members of the community feel welcome brought me to tears. At last I felt truly accepted.

The temple at Neasden wasn't the only one that moved to change its access policies after talking to me about my experiences with Kika. My message about the importance of access was reaching far and wide. On the back of the BBC Asian Network interview, I was approached by temples across the country. A number of temples in England as well as in the US and Canada adopted the training guidelines we came up with in London. I also met with a team from London City Hall, the home of the Greater London Authority, to talk about access issues more broadly.

Inspired by my story, the Shree Swaminarayan Temple in Streatham, a much smaller establishment than its big sister in Neasden, raised money for Guide Dogs. When Seema and I visited to thank them for their efforts, Kika walked right into the temple as though she owned the place. And this temple was comfortable with her being inside. Little by little, my faith in the world around me was being restored.

I was determined to spread the message further, engaging with people from all over the place on social media, encouraging them to try to change things in their own local places of worship. As I saw the practical changes that were being made as a result of my actions, I started to believe that I could make a wider difference. I could channel the energy I'd once put into my work as a doctor into activism. I realized that Kika hadn't just given me the confidence to get back out in the world, she'd given me the confidence to try to change it.

17

Finding My Way

Within a short period of time, Kika had already changed our lives in so many ways, but a much bigger change was on the horizon.

Since I'd lost my sight in November 2013, all the plans we'd made for our married life had been on hold. While we were coming to terms with what had happened, we certainly hadn't had time to think about children. For a long time we didn't feel ready for any next steps. I definitely wasn't ready for fatherhood. Seema already had to do so much for me. Losing my vision had turned me from a husband into a child again. How could I expect Seema to take on the burden of real childcare too? The stress of my sight loss had taken its physical toll on her as well, and she had started developing vitiligo, a condition where white patches appear on the skin, on her hands.

However, moving from Guildford to London had helped me to have more independence, and now with Kika by my side, I was taking new leaps forward every day. The more confident I became, the less stress Seema had to carry for the both of us. The less stress she had, the better she felt. The better she felt, the less the white patches of vitiligo spread. At last we dared to make real plans again and we decided those plans definitely included children. What we never dreamed to hope for was that we would fall pregnant so quickly. It was mid-December 2015, just over two years since that terrible day when I had woken up with blood on my pillow.

We took two tests to be sure. We sat cross-legged on the bathroom floor as Seema watched the blue cross appear on the stick. I held my breath.

'Are you ready for this?' she asked me.

I nodded.

'It's positive,' she said and I could hear the grin on her face.

Of course, we knew we would have more obstacles to overcome than the average set of first-time parents, but as soon as Seema told me the news, I knew it was meant to be.

At around the same time, Kika had reached a turning point with Seema, going from being ambivalent towards her at best to suddenly being very attentive. She'd started waiting by the door for Seema to come home in the evenings, running down the corridor to the lift when Seema came into the building. When Seema sat down on the floor to be with her, Kika had taken to resting her head on Seema's belly. Seema was delighted by this change in their relationship. 'See, she loves me now!' she said.

Now we understood what had brought about the change in Kika's attitude. Kika must have known that Seema was pregnant even before we did. Had she picked up on a shift in the balance in Seema's hormones?

The first scan made it real. It took place at the newly built antenatal centre at King's College Hospital. Kika came with us, of course. When the baby appeared on the screen and we heard the heartbeat, Kika nuzzled Seema's belly. Kika loved her little sibling before he or she was even born.

Discovering that Seema was pregnant coincided with another big life change for us. Though we'd been approved by Guide Dogs to have a dog in our Docklands flat, we'd always said that ideally we'd like a house with a proper garden where that dog would have its own space to run around in when it was off duty. As soon as we went on the waiting list for a guide dog, we also put our flat on the market, hoping that we might be settled into a new place by the time I found a match. But because I was matched with Kika so quickly, we hadn't yet had a chance to move. Soon, though, we found a buyer for the flat and started viewing houses further out from the centre, where we might be able to afford our own little patch of grass.

Naturally, when we were house-hunting, Kika came too. However, we found that some vendors preferred Kika to be left outside with the agent while Seema guided me around with the owners. Others would allow Kika into the house but not let us take her upstairs. We'd never know what the situation would be until we got there.

We saw dozens of houses. On paper, they all had potential, but none of them quite felt right. They just didn't feel like home. We kept looking for a place that fit all our require-ments: an open layout, easy access to public transport and that all-important garden. Then one weekend we agreed to view a place that didn't really fit our wish list at all. We'd been looking at houses with hundred-foot gardens and this one looked like a shoebox in comparison.

The vendors were not at home when we arrived, so the estate agent who took the viewing said it would be fine to let Kika off her harness. Just as when Kika first visited our flat in Docklands, as soon as she was free, she headed straight off to have a proper nose around. While Seema and I stood in the hallway talking to the agent, Kika went from room to room getting the measure of the place. When she'd finished looking at the ground floor, Kika stood at the bottom of the stairs and stared at Seema until Seema gave her the signal that it was OK to look upstairs too. Kika dashed up the stairs, did a quick tour of the bedrooms, then ran back down to the hallway and barked three times. After that, she ran up the stairs again and settled herself on the landing, with her paws draped over the top step, looking down at us.

By now we were used to the fact that Kika is not a very vocal dog; she's not a barker. Apparently, she didn't bark at all during training. Seema and I had heard her bark once when we took her to Southend and she encountered some other dogs on the beach, but other than that she hadn't said much. In that house in a corner of south-east London, however, Kika wanted us to hear exactly what she thought. Seema told me that Kika was grinning from ear to ear as she sat at the top of the stairs. That triple bark had been her vote of approval. This was the house for her.

When we'd first agreed to view this particular house, we'd been unsure it would be worth the trip because of the small garden. But Kika had chosen for us and it wasn't the garden that swung it for her, it was the landing – the perfect spot from which she could keep an eye on us all.

So we put in an offer. Kika liked the house, and luckily we did too, so it was the place for us. Apart from the dog-friendly landing, it had lots of other plus points. It was within walking distance of a train station that would make the commute into central London easy. There were plenty of shops and cafes nearby, not to mention a big park where Kika could let off steam. Our offer was accepted. We started to prepare for the move. Everything seemed to be going smoothly. We couldn't believe our luck. Until the day we were due to exchange contracts . . .

Our buyers announced that they wanted us to drop our price by a considerable amount. Enough to make it impossible for us to buy our new home. I was furious. We were ready to move. We wanted to be settled in long before the baby arrived in the summer. We had no idea at that point how hard or easy it would be for us to look after a newborn. The last thing we wanted was to lose the house that seemed so right and have to put the flat back on the market. So, with the help of our brilliant estate agent, who kept assuring us that our flat had gone up in value over the intervening months and would sell again very quickly if necessary, after a few hours on the phone and some very tough negotiations, we came to a conclusion: we refused to reduce the price of the flat but managed to secure the deal by leaving all our very nice, expensive furniture behind in lieu of a reduction. The buyers got a proper bargain. We got the house we wanted but, when we moved in, in January 2016, we had nothing but a mattress, a sofa and two dining chairs to our names!

Kika was happy, though. She had her special landing. She

made it her official spot and can often be found up there having a snooze when she's not at work. I don't think I've heard her bark since.

It was a busy spring.

Obviously, when I lost my sight, I lost my job. There was no way I could continue to work in A&E as a blind person. It was a terrible blow. My career as a doctor had meant so much to me. It had been my goal in life since I was eighteen years old. I'd put in seven years of hard study. I was good at it. To have it all end so suddenly was devastating.

When you can't do anything much, the days feel so long – there were long stretches of time when life just seemed boring and home could feel like a cage. I envied Seema her time at the office. I missed being busy. I missed having colleagues to banter with. I missed meeting new people all the time. I even missed the ones I'd previously considered to be a pain in the neck. If I'm honest, I also missed the prestige of being a practising doctor.

The RNIB Living with Sight Loss course was helpful not just because it addressed the practical problems of being visually impaired, but because it thrust me back into the world again. I had to meet new people and get to know them. I loved hearing their stories and turning strangers into friends. On the course I also learned about a government scheme to get disabled people back into work. In theory, it was a great idea. In practice, I made at least a hundred calls to the helpline in the hope of getting an appointment with a disability work advisor but had no luck whatsoever. It was so frustrating. I wanted to be doing something. So when an opportunity came along to help run the RNIB's Living with Sight Loss course alongside my friend Steve, whom I'd met on the London course, I jumped at it.

I was assigned a volunteer position on the Lewisham course. It took place over six weeks at the council offices and I could get the bus from the new house door to door. Which worked out great until the night I found myself on a bus that had to be taken out of service because of mechanical issues and I was dropped off in what might as well have been the middle of nowhere. Fortunately, a passer-by stopped to help and I made it home at last. A hungry Kika certainly wasn't pleased to be back so late.

Despite the transport hiccups, volunteering was another huge step on the road to independence. I was glad to be giving back again. It also gave me the confidence to pursue disability activism, perhaps as a full-time career, allowing me to further build on the success I'd had in getting the temple at Neasden to consider access for guide dogs.

To that end, I continued to get more active on social media, particularly Twitter. As well as running Kika's account, I now set up one for myself too. Kika's account had started with our training together, as a way for me to document my journey with a guide dog and share my experiences with family and friends, but it soon became a platform for engaging a wider and mainly non-disabled audience on the daily trials and tribulations of a working guide dog. My account provides a different perspective – not just the guide dog owner's view, but touching on issues that are important to me.

To tweet, I use the voiceover functionality that is part of the accessibility software built into iPhones. It reads out what is on the screen, so you can navigate apps without having to look at them. I use voiceover to dictate tweets and send them. Photos are more hit and miss. I take multiple shots and send them to Seema, who picks the best/clearest one that has everyone in the frame, then use that. When I was starting out, I wouldn't always know when the camera was facing me and Seema would just get ten different selfies that I had unwittingly taken in an attempt to get one good shot of Kika!

I was using Twitter as a platform to discuss the discrimination I experienced, but I wanted to share the good news too. One of my first tweets was about children's books in braille. In turn, especially after the media attention I'd received when I tackled the problems I'd encountered in the Neasden Temple, I was being sought out as a voice for accessibility reform.

That opened up some wonderful opportunities. In March 2016 I was invited to take part in a national campaign called Access All Areas, which focused on theatre accessibility week. I was interviewed by Channel 4's Cathy Newman and was featured alongside Matthew Perry, most famous for playing Chandler in *Friends*, who was in London for the opening of his dark comedy play *The End of Longing* at the Playhouse Theatre. It was great to meet him. He was very friendly and warm – Kika loved him and vice versa – and we had a few laughs during the recording. He told me he was very keen that the staff at his theatre should be trained to guide people correctly.

As we prepared for the recording, Perry admitted that he didn't know anything about guide dogs. I gave him a potted history and was very impressed when he memorized what

I'd told him and delivered the facts to the camera half an hour later as though he'd been working with guide dogs his whole life. I guess that's the skill that makes him a great actor.

Soon I was being given the opportunity to take centre stage too. The first time I read braille in public came thanks to the CEO of Guide Dogs at the time, Richard Leaman. He was speaking at an event and, following our interactions, thought I would be well placed to talk to the audience about the skills and talents that disabled persons can bring to a workforce. I had a month's notice to prepare a fifteen-minute speech.

The event took place at Westminster Boating Base, overlooking the River Thames. I had an audience of over a hundred people. I was used to talking to groups of people, having given presentations as a doctor, but it was disconcerting not to be able to see their faces and gauge how my speech was going down from their expressions. Now I had to read the room in a different way, listening for sounds of amusement or – though hopefully not – bored shuffling. Thankfully, I got some good laughs. The crowd was friendly and had been well primed by Richard. I was able to read my braille notes without skipping words through nerves. It all went well. It was another milestone and gave me the confidence to think I might actually be able to have a public speaking career. Richard's trust in me was a huge boost to my self-esteem.

Since Kika had changed my life so profoundly, I wanted to give back to Guide Dogs in whatever way I could. They enrolled me on a speaker-training course so that I could represent them at speaking engagements at schools, libraries, Scout and Guide groups and businesses all over London. I also helped Guide Dogs deliver talks to potential corporate donors – that is, organizations that were choosing their charities for the year and who we hoped would choose to sponsor a guide dog puppy. Telling my story to these varied audiences with Kika by my side was always emotional, because it was so raw, but I did it because I knew what a difference having a guide dog could make to someone else.

Gradually, I have come to advise corporations about their accessibility policies as a private consultant. It's not been without its challenges. Especially when it comes to getting paid. You would not believe the companies – huge household names – that have asked me and Kika to star in glossy corporate videos for no fee. I respond by asking if they think that someone with a disability should be grateful to be invited, or that they have nothing better to do than give up their time for free. The majority of companies have been very good, though, when it comes to understanding that my time is as good as anyone else's.

Getting back to work has made me value myself again. You don't realize how many of the things that add to your self-esteem are linked to work – confidence, colleagues, having a routine, how you dress . . .

As a hospital doctor, I was always clean-shaven and always wore a tailored suit. I'd go shopping once a quarter and stock up. I didn't own many casual clothes and certainly rarely got the chance to wear them. So it was a shock to find myself wearing pyjamas and joggers all day when I first lost my sight. Knowing I looked sloppy made me feel worse, so finding a new look for myself was an important part of regaining my identity.

First, I needed to get groomed. Newly blind, I found

shaving really hard and would cut myself all too often. Now, I have a perfectly shaped and trimmed beard, but learning to maintain it was quite something. Even after lots of practice, if I nick one side I'll never manage to get it straight again, so the whole beard has to come off and I start from scratch. Though you'll be relieved to know that my good Indian genes mean the beard is back within a week!

I'd had the same barber in Guildford for years, but when we moved to London, I'd had to run the gauntlet of trying to find someone new to take on my hair. I suffered some terrible haircuts along the way, at one point – much to Seema's horror – coming home with a crew cut despite having paid fancy London prices for something more sophisticated.

Then, while I was training with Kika in the early days, someone from the RNIB recommended a barber's called Chaplin's, which was a little further out in Deptford, but apparently worth the trip. It was a DLR journey with a few changes and also involved crossing a busy junction, so we made it part of our training to find our way there. My RNIB friend was right. It was a long way to go just to get a haircut but the barber was brilliant, sorted my hair and could fix my beard when needed. Well worth the trip. And Kika learned the route like a pro. It was another one to add to her ever-increasing list!

Having once been so fashion-conscious, when it came to clothes I was now reliant on Seema. A major step in accepting my new situation was letting go of my old suits, which only served to remind me of the life I would no longer have. On clear-out day, Seema took about fifteen Savile Row suits to a charity shop in Guildford. I was heartbroken. But she also came home with new clothes – chinos, jeans and jumpers –

for me to try. At the time, nothing felt very much like 'me', but who was I anyway? Jeans felt particularly strange. It's taken me years to get comfortable in them.

In the end, clothes were easy enough to find, especially with a wife who loves shopping, but everything else was harder. I was (and still am) super particular about shoes – too thick a sole and I couldn't feel the tactile paving under my feet sufficiently, too thin and they were uncomfortable. I wanted something stylish that wasn't a sports trainer or black leather work shoe. I went through a lot of styles until I found a brand that worked. Now I buy those in multiples too.

I'm always discussing accessible design with regard to buildings and transport in my talks to businesses, but the same principles apply to technology and fashion. If it's fashionable, it's usually impractical, and if it's accessible, it tends to be ugly. It can feel as though people expect us just to be grateful that there are accessible products out there at all. But why can't those products be accessible *and* stylish? Take, for example, telling the time. It's easy when you wear a watch – you can take a quick discreet glance down during a meeting and no one is any the wiser. Try doing that when you're visually impaired and the whole room will know what time it is, thanks to your 1980s-style digital speaking watch. Standard issue for any blind person, they are also ugly as hell.

What are the alternatives? A smart watch? The constant wearing of headphones? They're not always safe. I was concerned that the visible use of technology in public places would make me a target for thieves. The watch thing frustrated me so much. I researched to no avail and even wrote to a large number of watch manufacturers to ask whether they had any tactile models. I wanted a proper watch, not another piece of technology, but there was nothing out there. Thankfully, Seema discovered a company in the US that had just started to make tactile watches. I still had to wait a good few years before I could get my hands on one but I now wear it with pride. It's a beautiful-looking timepiece, a great conversation starter and is inclusive design personified. But more simply, it's just nice to wear a proper watch again.

The way I look is important to me. It always was. As a doctor, I understood the power of dressing the part. When I had on my white coat it was a signal that I knew what I was doing and people trusted me. I understand that just because I can no longer see what I look like, it doesn't mean that people seeing me won't continue to respond to the cues they get from the way I dress and hold myself. Just because I'm blind doesn't mean that I don't want to look good.

So I dress to impress. Knowing I look professional gives me confidence and authority. I'm aware that when I'm dressed down, people treat me differently. Having spent those few miserable weeks in pyjamas and joggers, one of the best things about getting back to work again was having an excuse to put on a suit.

18

A New Arrival

Before our baby was born, Seema and I were very anxious as to how we would cope with the reality of having a child. What roles would we each play? How much would I be able to do for the baby? I very much wanted to be a hands-on dad, so we spent months researching everything – from buggies to carriers to clothing.

We spent whole days in baby-related shops testing prams, baby carriers and car seats, working out how many changing mats we needed, deciding whether a nappy bin was an essential, et cetera, et cetera. It was overwhelming. My lack of sight meant we needed the things we bought to be easy for me to use. Even finding a baby monitor that was straightforward and tactile enough was not a simple task.

Baby clothes were a potential area of difficulty. So many Babygros have fiddly poppers that are hard enough to do up when you can see them and next to impossible when you can't. When we found out that in America it was the norm to have practical zips instead of those silly little poppers, we immediately stocked up, despite the shipping costing just as much as the onesies.

Choosing a car seat was also tough. Trying to fit the seat into the Isofix base is a puzzle for any new parent. I needed it to feel solid and robust when it fitted into place. Visual indicators such as green lights were useless for me. I was relying on hearing that heavy 'click'. We found the right seat eventually but I still needed to add more tactile indicators to locate where it needed to be placed on the base.

But the ultimate challenge was finding the right buggy. How do you push a buggy while holding on to a guide dog harness? How was I going to do that? Early on in the pregnancy, Seema and I made a special trip to Mothercare to look at the options.

I'd quickly worked out that pushing a buggy while hanging on to Kika was not going to work, though *pulling* a buggy just might. However, if you've ever tried pulling a regular buggy or stroller, you quickly realize that you can't steer it that way. This is because the smaller wheels, which pivot in the direction you want to go, end up at the back while the fixed wheels end up at the front. This makes it difficult to manoeuvre. Just being able to flip the handle would leave the wheels in the same position, allowing you to pull the buggy and manoeuvre it.

Unfortunately, those of us who really need to be able pull a buggy are in the minority and that was reflected in the choices presented to us on our research trip. I think I even managed to break a few prams while trying them out. We found only one that had a proper flip handle. It was a Bugaboo, the brand beloved of London's most fashionable parents and far from the cheapest option. But if I wanted to be actively involved in every aspect of our baby's life, a Bugaboo it would have to be. This was our biggest baby purchase by a long way. It took up much more of the baby budget than we'd originally anticipated and meant we would have to make sacrifices elsewhere. It made me worry that we'd have to spend so much more to get the baby kit that might be accessible for me.

We definitely needed a special buggy, and finding the zip-up Babygros was a boon, but as we prepared for our new arrival, we actually discovered that most of the equipment we needed did not have to be specifically designed for the visually impaired. It was more important for us to establish those military-style routines and for me to know exactly where the things I needed would be. After all, Seema would be there to make sure I didn't put a nappy on backwards!

Like many soon-to-be parents, we also had to rejig things in the house to better accommodate our impending arrival. I know my way around our home and can navigate it easily without sight, so long as things are where I expect them to be. Seema understands the importance of everything having its place. There is no impromptu tidying out of cupboards or rearranging surfaces and storage without us doing it together, otherwise I won't find things. In the seven months since moving in, I'd arranged our new house in a way that suited my needs, but now my office was going to be the nursery. It was where Kika and I spent most of our days, but now she needed to learn not to go into that room without our permission, which was quite the change.

The other unknown was how Kika would react to our new arrival – would she feel threatened? How would she behave? All dogs are different, and even with her calm temperament, we couldn't really know how Kika might respond. That said, Kika had come with us to every single scan and hospital appointment. Her ears would prick up every time she heard the little heartbeat and she would always be by Seema's side during the scan.

Throughout the spring and summer, whenever she wasn't at work with me, Kika stayed as close to Seema as she was able. As she followed Seema around the house, with her big doggy eyes full of adoration, it was hard to believe that she had ever been ambivalent towards my darling wife. Kika's devotion was complete. We were quietly hopeful that her feelings would extend to the baby when he or she finally arrived.

The hospital was used to seeing Kika at antenatal appointments, but our biggest fear was how we could manage her while Seema was in labour. We had no idea how long labour would last; we could end up being in hospital for days, in which case, who would look after Kika?

We'd never left Kika alone and she'd never really been apart from both of us at the same time. She'd have to come with us. Thus the next important step in preparation for the baby's arrival was to do a tour of the hospital's birth centre to ensure I knew where we were going and to introduce ourselves and Kika to the team. We were anxious to get them all comfortable with our needs, but this was actually something we didn't need to worry about at all. The midwives at the birth centre were incredibly welcoming. There were no restrictions regarding Kika, which massively put our minds at ease.

The one thing we had no control over was how Kika would cope while Seema was in labour, so we planned for every eventuality. Kika could sit in the midwives' office if she got distressed and the grandparents were on call to pick her up if needed. As it happened, none of our contingency plans were needed.

As the day approached everything began to slot into place. I called our local taxi company to advise them that we'd need their services to get to the hospital and that we would have a guide dog with us. This isn't something I would normally do – the law states that taxis and minicabs have a duty to carry guide and other assistance dogs at no extra cost so it shouldn't be an issue at all – but assistance dogs are very often refused by cab drivers and this wasn't a risk we wanted to take at such an important time.

All mums-to-be are advised to pack their hospital bags when they hit thirty-six weeks pregnant. At our thirty-six-week mark, Seema packed her bag, a Kika bag and a bag for me too. Kika had a bowl, her bed, a toy and spare food, and in the bag for me? Snacks! And lots of them! Like I said, who knew how long the labour could last and how long we might be stuck in hospital . . .

Seema's due date came and went, but in the interim we enjoyed the summer, taking Kika out for extra walks and making the most of our time as a family of three before we hit the inevitable sleepless nights. It was a beautiful summer's evening when Seema went into labour. She managed for quite a long time at home, bouncing on her gym ball until her contractions were close enough together to justify going into hospital. I duly called the taxi and waited patiently at the door with our bags as Seema paced around the house. When the taxi arrived, we all piled in and were quickly at the hospital. Throughout the labour, which took place in a birthing pool just as Seema had planned, the midwives gave a running commentary on Seema's progress for my benefit. As a trainee doctor, I'd delivered several babies on one of my rotations, so I knew exactly what was supposed to be happening at any given moment. I sat close by and held Seema's hand.

Meanwhile, Kika wandered the room as though she were an anxious expectant parent herself, occasionally resting her head on the side of the pool right next to Seema and looking at her with big brown eyes full of concern. If Kika could have spoken, I'm sure she'd have been giving Seema plenty of encouragement. She was the ultimate comfort. Kika stayed with us for the duration, helping to keep Seema calm and relaxed, even through the night when she (and we) would normally be sleeping soundly.

Within a few hours of arriving at the hospital our baby was born. Kika was right there as our son – her little brother, as we hoped she would come to think of him – came into the world. I cut the umbilical cord, with a bit of help from Daisy, the midwife. Daisy placed the baby in Seema's arms and I felt a rush of love unlike anything I'd ever felt before.

'We made a little person,' Seema said.

After all those months of waiting and planning and, if I'm honest, worrying, I was overwhelmed with emotion.

'Would Dad like to hold the baby?' asked Daisy. I immediately made myself comfortable in an armchair.

I was holding my son in my arms at last. I'd never felt such a rush of pure happiness. But I still found time for a joke.

'Does he look like me?' I asked one of the midwives.

The midwife became a little awkward but Seema, thankfully, knew it was just my warped sense of humour. And she also knew that beyond the joke I really did want to know what my son looked like. Tenderly, Seema described him to me – his hair (or lack of it), his squishy nose, pink face, long fingers and chubby feet; the fact that he had come out with one hand on his cheek. As I held him, he still had his hand on his cheek. Seema said he looked perfectly relaxed in my arms. He'd been born calm. He didn't cry.

'Now he's looking at you,' Seema told me as he opened his eyes.

It was at that moment that I was struck by all the things I would never share with my son. No matter how well Seema described him to me, I'd never know for sure what he looked like. I'd never be able to look into his eyes as he looked into mine. I'd never be able to teach him how to drive, as my father had taught me. But holding him then made me more determined than ever that he should not miss out on anything because of my blindness. I made a silent promise that I would be the very best father I could be and our son would never hear me say, 'You can't do that because I'm blind.'

We were very lucky that everything went smoothly with the baby's arrival and felt blessed that Kika was there throughout. The first opportunity she got, Kika came over to check out the baby and gave him a good sniff. She had been so serene during the labour, and it set the tone for her relationship with her little brother from the off. She was his protector and loved him already, we could tell.

We soaked up this moment of bliss before quickly realizing that we hadn't told anyone in the family that we were in hospital and that the baby had arrived! It was time to make some calls.

We named our son Abhishek – Abhi for short.

One of the best things about that day was ringing everyone up to let them know that Abhi had arrived. It was a real thrill to call Mum and Dad and tell them, 'I am holding an amazing little boy in my arms . . .' They were with us within the hour.

Neither Kika nor I had slept the whole time we were at the hospital. Kika had not left Seema's side and, once Abhi arrived, she still considered herself on duty. When one of the nurses tried to take Abhi away to get him cleaned up, Kika actually blocked her exit. She took some persuading to let the baby out of her sight. It was only when the nurse brought Abhi back to the room that Kika finally relaxed and allowed herself a little snooze.

A few hours later, Dad took Kika and me home to get freshened up, leaving Seema and the baby at the hospital to rest a bit longer. It was the strangest feeling leaving them there but I was so excited to get the house ready for their welcome home. On the way out of the hospital, I was stopped by a familiar voice. It was our midwife Harriet, who had done all of Seema's antenatal appointments. She was thrilled to hear the news of the baby's arrival. I didn't have to say a word, to be honest, my ridiculous grin despite a night of no sleep immediately gave away the happy news.

It wasn't long before we were all back home again – the next day, in fact – and in at the deep end. Seema and I carried Abhi into the house in his car seat and set him down in the middle of the living room. We sat on the floor to either side of him, just marvelling at our luck. Meanwhile, now that the baby seat was on her level, Kika put her nose right into it, getting her first proper sniff of her little bro. He didn't seem in the slightest bit worried as she gently nosed at him. It was as though Abhi understood from the start that Kika was going to look after him as though he were her own.

And so we came to our first night at home with our son. We'd had months of preparation for this moment but all the same, we were stunned and a little shell-shocked. We had our baby at last. What now?

Seema did the first nappy change. As she did so, Abhi started weeing straight up into the air. Neither of us had planned for that. *Welcome to parenthood*, we thought.

I was in awe of our little man, but the first few weeks of having a new baby at home were quite a shock for us. I'd started to use the changing unit that I'd set up downstairs and was getting more and more confident in looking after him in the house, but Abhi cried a lot and we couldn't work out why. Did he have colic? Wind? Was he too hot? Too cold? Even the midwives weren't sure what was going on. Our stress levels were going through the roof. Combine that with sleep deprivation and we were not in a happy place.

To make things worse, we then found out that Abhi was dehydrated and jaundiced because, unbeknown to us, he wasn't feeding properly. This went some way to explaining his crying but, needless to say, it devastated Seema, who had been doing everything possible to feed him. It made me feel useless too. We went back and forth to the hospital, where poor Abhi had to have loads of blood tests in the search for a diagnosis. We were advised to start with a feeding plan – Seema should continue to breastfeed, to pump in between feeds and to top him up with formula – but we still didn't know what was wrong.

It took a few visits to a breastfeeding support group before he was eventually diagnosed with a tongue-tie, which is where the strip of skin connecting the baby's tongue to the floor of their mouth is shorter than usual. This can restrict the tongue's movement, making it harder to breastfeed. It's not always easy to spot and often only becomes apparent when the baby has problems feeding. This was the reason why he wasn't able to feed efficiently, wasn't gaining weight and was dehydrated. It was a huge relief to know the cause of Abhi's distress, but it would be a few more weeks before we could get an appointment to have it cut. Until then, Seema persevered and I helped with the bottles. Putting all the fiddly parts together, pouring out the formula and getting it to the right temperature was another challenge that I took on with gusto.

The day came for Abhi's tongue-tie to be cut. It's a very simple procedure, but to have it done we had to travel to a hospital in central London by public transport. We were advised not to feed Abhi for a few hours before so that he would be hungry enough to breastfeed straight afterwards. The enzymes in Seema's breast milk would help to soothe any pain from the cut. Easier said than done. Because Abhi was still very tiny, we'd found that feeding him little and often worked well, but this wasn't helpful on the day of his procedure.

We tried to time it perfectly – a feed, straight into the buggy, onto a train, a ten-minute walk to the hospital and straight to his appointment. Five minutes into our train journey he was crying inconsolably. By this point it was too close to his scheduled appointment time to feed him again, so the best we could do was to try to comfort him. But his piercing cry alongside the lack of sleep did little for our stress levels and made the twenty-minute journey into central London feel like a lifetime. We pinned our hopes on the fresh air and brisk walk to the hospital to help him fall asleep but alas that didn't work either. At the hospital, Abhi joined the cacophony of other screaming babies waiting to be seen. Fortunately, we didn't have to wait long, but we were caught off-guard by what came next.

The consultant's office was the size of a shoebox. We had to leave the buggy outside. It had a desk and a couple of chairs for the consultant and Seema, who was holding Abhi. I stood in the corner with a specialist nurse. Kika sat by Seema's feet. The consultant confirmed Abhi's details, took a look inside his mouth and then asked to take a photo. Of course we said 'yes'. Through all of this, Abhi was still crying. Then the consultant performed the procedure, which took seconds. Afterwards, Seema fed Abhi as planned. It took an hour to calm him down.

As we headed home, Seema told me what had really gone on in the consultant's office that day. What I hadn't realized is that when the consultant asked to take a photo, it wasn't a picture of Abhi's tongue-tie as I had presumed, but of Kika. There's a time and a place for these things. Seema hadn't told me at the time because she knew I would be angry. She was correct. Right then, our focus was on Abhi.

Once Abhi's tongue-tie was cut, he quickly settled into a proper routine and we could relax a little more, although sleep was still off the agenda. Even Kika seemed relieved once he'd settled down. Seeing Abhi's baby thighs get chubby gave Seema and me the additional reassurance that we needed: Abhi was OK. And we were doing OK too.

Kika & Me

Those early days were very much about survival. We took things one day at a time. I had so much to learn still and my confidence with Abhi was improving all the time, but the general dad frustrations were compounded by not being able to deal with all these challenges in the way a sighted person would.

Our mantra throughout was, and still remains, that we would always find a way around things together. It may not be conventional, it may take me (us) a little longer, require a little (a lot) more thought, preparation and planning, but we get there in the end. This approach has served us well with everything – from the day to day of looking after a new baby, to taking a toddler out, to doing the grocery shopping and even to going on holiday as a family. I want my son to have an ordinary childhood, not be restricted as to what he can or can't do because his father is visually impaired. This is what drove – and continues to drive – my determination to live a 'normal' life and do everyday things independently.

And there were magical moments. I remember one special night feed. It was 4 a.m. when Abhi let us know that he wanted to be fed. Leaving Seema to rest, I crept downstairs, found the pumped milk and warmed the bottle up in some hot water. Then I sat down on the bedroom floor with Abhi in my arms and gave him the bottle. That's when Kika got out of her bed and came to join us. She nestled her heavy head in my lap and gazed at the little boy who had changed our world. When Abhi made the slightest noise of protest, Kika responded as if to comfort him by pressing her big nose against his little legs, letting him know she was right there beside him. It was the middle of the night and I was as bone-tired as only the parent of a newborn can be, but I had never felt so happy.

186

19

More Baby Steps

When Abhi was just six weeks old, Seema and I went into the city to support National Guide Dogs Week. I already knew I wanted to share our new parent happiness with other visually impaired people who might be wondering if parenting was a possibility for them. The best way to do that was to show everyone how well Seema and I had been getting on, so we decided we would take Abhi with us and make the event a family outing. He was still very small, and being well aware of the challenges of taking a large buggy into central London at rush hour where there might be steps to negotiate, I decided to carry him in his chest harness.

The trip into London went well, better than we had expected, in fact. Everyone was thrilled to meet our baby and Abhi seemed to enjoy himself, making happy little noises as the other guests cooed over him. Kika had a good time too, wagging her tail all evening long. I felt so proud to be able to show off my little family. However, the day took a turn for the worse when we were on our way home again.

At the train station, we had to take an escalator to get to the platform. I still had Abhi on my chest, one hand on the rail and the other on Kika's harness.

Escalator etiquette in London is something that people get

very exercised about. The general rule is to stand on the right so that people who want to walk up or down the escalator can get past on the left. Clearly, though, this isn't possible when travelling on an escalator with a guide dog. As always, Kika was standing beside me on my left-hand side as she had been trained to do and Seema was a couple of steps behind us. We were about halfway up when I heard footsteps quickly ascending the escalator behind me and, before I knew it, a woman was right there at my shoulder, asking me to move so she could get past.

I quickly explained that I couldn't move. I had to wait until we reached the top of the escalator before Kika and I could get out of the way. To do otherwise would be too dangerous, especially since I had Abhi in his harness on my front.

The woman didn't take it well. Never mind the safety of me, my son and Kika. When she heard my explanation, she snarled, 'Because of your dog, I'm going to miss my train.' I told her, perhaps a little sarcastically I'm afraid, 'I'm sorry my blindness is inconveniencing you,' but I still couldn't move to let her by. Though even had I been able to, I wouldn't have wanted to by this point. The woman continued to rant about how selfish I was until Seema got involved, putting the woman straight about her priorities.

It was a horrible confrontation. And pointless. As it happened, the woman didn't miss her train after all – Seema saw her boarding a carriage with plenty of time to spare – but her impatience cast a nasty shadow over our happy evening out as a family.

I'd become used to the bad manners Kika and I sometimes

experienced from other commuters who thought their journey was more important than my safety. I could take it. But how would I cope with the same ignorance and unkindness when I was out alone with Kika and Abhi when Seema wasn't there to back me up? What was it going to be like when I was holding Kika's harness and pulling the buggy at the same time? Would my plan to be a hands-on dad, doing my bit in every part of Abhi's life, just put my son in unnecessary danger? When we got home, Seema did her best to reassure me that she had no doubt whatsoever that I would be able to handle everything fatherhood threw at me, but that woman on the escalator had rattled my confidence.

Over the next few days, I mulled it over, checking that I wasn't being selfish and putting my determination to be the best dad ahead of our son's safety. I went over that incident on the escalator again and again. Was I at fault? Was it fair on Abhi or Kika to put them in that situation? In the end, with Seema's help, I came to the conclusion that there was no way I should let one ignorant commuter derail my plan to parent Abhi the way I wanted to and, in doing so, prove to myself and to him that my blindness was no limitation.

But I wasn't delusional. I knew that when it came to getting around with the buggy, I needed to put in plenty of practice with Seema alongside me to make sure Abhi came to no harm when we ventured out without her.

We started in the park near home – a safe place where I could learn to wrangle a buggy and Kika's harness without having to worry about traffic. Fortunately, as soon as the buggy came into the equation, Kika seemed to understand that she needed to help me out. Straight away, she changed her speed. She slowed right down to make sure that I was able to manoeuvre the buggy properly and, Seema told me, also made it her business to keep looking back and checking on the buggy to make sure that it was still there.

We practised walking around the park until having both my hands full started to feel natural and I was sure I could steer the buggy with ease. It was physically exhausting, but in no time at all I could manoeuvre that buggy like it was a dancing partner. Seema's belief in me and in Kika gave me the confidence I needed to be the dad I wanted to be.

It wasn't long before Diwali came around again. Seema and I were very excited at the thought of taking Abhi to the temple in Neasden for his very first experience of the festival. Thanks to Kika and our battle to get the temple to take assistance animals seriously, we knew that all the access issues had been solved and we could look forward to the visit with confidence.

At the temple, Kika luxuriated in her special bed in the security office, enjoying the attention of the security team, while I carried Abhi around the shrines in his harness. It was an emotional moment. In the space of three years, I had gone from losing my sight and my faith to walking into the temple with my head held high as I carried my infant son. I felt like every prayer I'd ever made had been answered. It was the best Diwali ever.

The next day, Seema and I visited her family in Preston and took Abhi to be blessed at the temple there too. The Preston temple had followed the story of what happened in Neasden closely, so they were also well prepared for our visit. They provided a bed, a water bowl and even a nice new chew toy for Kika. I was happy to leave her in the temple foyer to enjoy these kind gifts with the temple volunteers while Seema and I took Abhi to meet the priest.

We were very excited to be introducing Abhi to the temple that had been such a big part of Seema's early life. Alas, Abhi wasn't quite so keen on the whole experience and he soon began to cry. While we were trying to comfort him and dry his tears, Kika somehow escaped her chaperones and raced straight to find her baby brother. She must have heard him crying and decided she had to find out what was going on. There was no way Kika was going to let Abhi get upset on her watch. Seema watched in astonishment as Kika ran right past the priest into the temple's innermost room in search of her baby brother. She would not be stopped or diverted until she knew for sure that Abhi was safe.

As soon as Kika reached Abhi's side, she had a quick sniff of him and then sat herself down on the floor next to his car seat. Needless to say, the priest and other temple staff and worshippers were horrified, but fortunately they were so shocked that they were also speechless! Seema jumped into action, calming the priest and quickly leading Kika back to her bed in the foyer.

Kika doesn't care about any religious dogma. All that matters to her is the safety and happiness of the people she loves. In many ways, it seems to me that Kika's devotion to Abhi, Seema and me is what most religions are supposed to be about. Perhaps in years to come, it will be common to see a guide dog walk its owner right into the temple itself. I hope so.

Then all of a sudden it was January and Abhi was five months old. Seema was still on maternity leave but had to pop into the office to bring herself up to speed with what was going on in her absence. She decided to catch up with colleagues over a drink afterwards too. This was the first time that I would be looking after Abhi alone. I agreed that it was a good idea.

Throughout December I'd been laid low with a chest infection, but by the time January rolled around, I told Seema that I was more than ready to look after Abhi while she enjoyed a solo evening out for the first time since his birth. When she left for the office at three in the afternoon, I had no reservations about spending the evening alone. Seema was very happy to have the opportunity to dress up, go out and have some fun with her colleagues. She deserved a proper night out and I was looking forward to the opportunity of some one-to-one time with my son.

The afternoon went fine but by 6 p.m., I was feeling slightly less well. I could tell I had the beginnings of a temperature. Unable to summon the energy to do much else, I sat on the floor in the living room with Abhi on my lap, while Kika lay with her head across my ankles. After a while, I got up and put Abhi in his crib. As I did so, I felt a little dizzy. I put it down to being tired – what new parent isn't? – and perhaps I was more anxious than I had admitted about being home alone with the baby for the first time.

I pushed on through, but by seven o'clock, I was feeling much, much worse. I slumped on the sofa. Kika rested her head on my knee and I felt her watching with concern. My temperature was raging and my head was aching. I didn't know what to do. I didn't want to call Seema and interrupt her one night out in months. That didn't seem fair. At the same time, I knew that the responsible thing – the only thing – to do was to get her to come home so that if something serious were to happen to me, she would be there for Abhi and Kika.

I racked my doctor's brain for the right answer. What would I have told a patient to do under the same circumstances? Pop a couple of painkillers and soldier on? No way. Not if they were in sole charge of a baby. I would have advised them not to take the risk, of course. Abhi's safety had to be my priority. I called Seema.

Seema knew I wouldn't call her unless something serious was going on. Though at first she joked that she couldn't leave me alone for a minute, I could tell she was immediately concerned. I told her how I was feeling. By now I could barely even stand up straight. My balance was off. Seema told me she'd be on her way at once, but she was still forty-five minutes away.

When I got off the phone, Abhi started crying. I picked him up from his crib to comfort him and just about managed to keep it together until Seema walked in. All the time, Kika kept an anxious watch over the baby and me. As soon as Seema was inside, I handed Abhi over to her and fainted in the hallway. Kika didn't leave my side for a moment. Seema called for an ambulance and I was taken straight to hospital – to the Princess Royal, where Abhi was born.

While I was undergoing a series of tests to find out why my health had deteriorated so quickly, Mum and Dad came to the rescue again. Since Kika couldn't come with me to the

Princess Royal this time, they took her home with them so that Seema could concentrate on Abhi and me.

That night was the first Kika and I had spent apart since she came home with me from the training course in Redbridge – she'd been my constant companion. My parents told me that, suddenly separated from me, she sat by the front door of their house in Guildford all night long. She wouldn't go to bed. It was obvious that she was worried about me.

When it became clear that, whatever was wrong, I was going to have to be in hospital for a while, we knew we had to make other plans. Kika was finding it hard to settle while I wasn't at home and we didn't want her to get distressed or for this enforced time apart to undo months' worth of bonding and training. Kika needed to be able to come and see me. I was moved to King's College Hospital where she was able to visit every day. She would sit next to my bed with her chin on the mattress, looking at me with the same concern she'd shown while Seema was in the birthing suite.

A series of tests showed that I'd had a kidney infection. It was the first of three such infections over the course of a year that sent me to hospital each time. The doctors could find no reason why I reacted so badly other than that my immune system was over-reactive. It was frustrating to say the least. All I wanted was to be with Seema, Abhi and Kika, moving ahead with our lives. We were all relieved when I came home at last.

20

The Fairy Dog-Mother

While Abhi was tiny and I could carry him around or know that when I put him down, he wasn't going to go anywhere, he was relatively easy to wrangle. When it came to changing him, I'd quickly worked out that playing music helped to calm him down. Nappy-changing was one of the toughest things I'd had to get my head around as a new parent. As soon as Abhi was born, I threw myself into the deep end and insisted on doing a nappy change solo. Of course it was a poo nappy but, just like Seema, the thing I really wasn't prepared for was the 'fountain' that came mid-change. As parents of boys will know, it's an occupational hazard. I had to use at least half a packet of wipes during one change to make sure both Abhi and I were clean afterwards. But practice makes perfect and after a while I found it easy. From early on, it also seemed to me that Abhi reacted very differently when it was me who was changing him rather than Seema. When he was with me, he kicked and wriggled less as though he knew he needed to help me out. Perhaps Kika had passed the message on to him.

After making sure that I had the nappy on the right way round, the second hardest thing for me was learning to get the tension of the nappy right. I definitely didn't want to get it too tight, but too loose and it would fall off as soon as Abhi started moving.

Before we knew it, crawling was on the agenda. I had been putting off the question: what do I do when he starts to crawl? It's a moment every doting parent looks forward to but, at the same time, I knew it was going to bring with it a whole new raft of challenges for me. If I couldn't see where Abhi was or what he was doing, how on earth could I make sure he was safe? What if he got up the stairs? What if he crawled into the garden? What if he somehow managed to find his way out of the front door? But as with so many things, the answer lay with Kika.

Kika is not always on duty as a guide dog. There are times when she is just allowed to be an ordinary dog and enjoy a run around in the park with her canine friends. When I take her out to the park purely for exercise and for fun, she's allowed off the harness and I put a bell on her collar so that I can more easily work out where she is when it's time to put the harness back on and go home.

The bell is Kika's favourite signal. If we're leaving the house and she hears me put the bell in my pocket, she knows exactly where we are going and her pace of walking and the speed of her tail wags increase in line with her excitement. The system works so well – my ears are finely attuned to the sound of Kika's bell – that I decided I would try it with Abhi too. I'd put a bell on our son so that when he was on the move I could always tell where he was. Seema agreed it was a very good idea, if slightly wacky.

Luckily, Abhi didn't seem to mind that as he was learning to crawl he jangled like a mountain goat on the hillside. The sleigh-bell sound of Abhi's little bell became a joyful noise to me, meaning as it did that he was growing and changing just as he ought to be. There was nothing better than hearing that bell jingling fast as Abhi got up some speed across the carpet, followed by the sound of his laughter. The bell gave him his freedom and me much needed peace of mind.

Kika always did her best to help too. When Abhi was learning to toddle, he flatly refused to use the baby walker we had chosen with such care. He preferred instead to hang on to Kika's collar and walk around using her as his support. When Kika wasn't in harness and helping me, she became Abhi's personal assistance animal.

Kika didn't mind. She was endlessly patient with her little bro. She was always gentle and passive when he grabbed her ears, tweaked her nose or stuck his little fist in her mouth. She didn't even complain when Abhi once shoved a twig between her teeth while she was sleeping. Likewise she never sulked if we were giving Abhi all our attention. She was never jealous or upset. Abhi was as precious to Kika as he was to Seema and me. Despite the worries we'd had when Becca warned us that Kika found bonding tricky, she was absolutely part of the family now. Because of that, she made our lives easy.

Kika got involved with every aspect of Abhi's daily routine. As well as for the obvious practical reasons, I'd learned to read braille so that I could enjoy the pleasure of having books in my life again. With the arrival of Abhi, the skill I'd gone to such pains to perfect when we were living in the Docklands really came into its own. Books had been an important part of my childhood. When I was small, the bedtime stories my parents read to me were a highlight of my day and helped to foster my later love of learning. I wanted that to be the case for Abhi too.

Of course, Seema could have taken charge of the bedtime routine, but having done my time changing stinky nappies, I was determined not to miss out on all the perks of fatherhood. I wanted to be able to read to my son. So I was thrilled when someone told me about Clearvision, an initiative working out of a school in Wimbledon, which transcribes children's books into braille. Even picture books. You want *The Very Hungry Caterpillar* with braille captions? You got it.

I signed up for Clearvision's loan scheme and every couple of weeks they send me new books to read to Abhi. I don't know which one of us was more excited. It wasn't long before Kika got in on the act too. Now, whenever I'm reading Abhi a story at the end of the day, Kika always makes sure she's right there in the audience alongside her little bro and an ever-increasing array of stuffed animals. We all sit together on the bedroom floor.

Seema tells me that both Abhi and Kika enjoy listening to a good book, though Kika seems to find some of the stories soporific. It's never long before I feel her rest her heavy head on my knee. When she starts snoring – she has a very impressive snore – we know it's time for Abhi to get under the covers and say goodnight.

With the passing years, Kika and Abhi's bond grows ever closer. They simply adore one another. Theirs is a very special relationship. It's no exaggeration to say that we would not have Abhi were it not for Kika. She is not just Abhi's big sister, she is his fairy dog-mother.

*

From the day Abhi was born, we wanted him to grow up feeling as though the world is his oyster, so when he was nine months old, we decided it was time to take our first family holiday abroad. Of course Kika would be coming with us. It would be her first flight too.

Booking a flight with a guide dog isn't always easy. For a start, you need to plan well ahead since there are limited spaces for assistance dogs on most flights. Policies vary from airline to airline. Fortunately, Seema took charge.

Unlike most animals, which have to travel in the hold, Kika comes in the cabin with us when we fly. She gets a seat of her own, though she doesn't sit on it but on the floor beneath it. We can't be in the emergency exit seats but we usually save up and splash out on premium seats so that Kika has plenty of room.

One of the questions I'm asked most frequently is how I deal with Kika needing to relieve herself in mid-air. In order to make sure that Kika doesn't need the loo while we're travelling, we have to work out very carefully when she'll be fed ahead of the flight. It's not the most fun for Kika, who loves her food as much as the next Labrador and gets grumpy when it's slow in coming, and it's a nightmare if the flight is delayed, but mostly it's been OK. Airports also have special areas where assistance dogs can take a pee before boarding.

Seema and I don't exactly travel light but Kika is something else. We have to take her bed, her kit and all her food with us. It takes up a lot of our luggage allowance.

For our first trip abroad with Abhi and Kika, we chose to go to Malta in May – it wasn't too far away, there were beaches and history there, and, primarily, we thought it wouldn't be too hot at that time of year. Extreme heat not only makes it difficult for Kika to work, given that she is not used to it, but it isn't great for a baby either. The weather was forecast to be in the mid-twenties while we were there, but within a day of our arrival, it had already gone up to thirty degrees, which was frustrating. We had to make sure Kika stayed in the shade and drank plenty of water. However, even if the weather wasn't as predictable as we hoped, Kika's first flight went well. She was very calm about being on the plane. So long as she could keep an eye on me and Abhi she was happy.

Our plan was to have a normal family holiday and do normal things that normal families do, like spend time by the pool, go sightseeing, find the nicest beaches and hunt for the best ice cream. We stayed at the Corinthia Hotel and they really couldn't have worked harder to make us feel welcome. They'd never had a guide dog guest before but they did their research to ensure that Kika would be as comfortable as their human guests. We arrived to find that the hotel had upgraded us to a suite to give us extra space. They'd furnished it with a dog bed, bowls, treats and toys for Kika. They'd thought about Abhi as well. They'd set up a cot in the bedroom and provided toys and storybooks for his amusement too.

Malta was an easy place to start our family travel adventures, especially because we were able to visit an old family friend. Added to that, nearly all the people we met spoke at least some English and they were charmed to meet Kika.

The first week of our Malta trip was great. Unfortunately, during the second week, I became ill with a repeat of the kidney infection that had laid me low when Seema made her

Kika is always by my side, regardless of where we are. Her favourite thing to do when we're travelling is to rest her head on my knee.

A surprise visit back to the Guide Dogs training centre at Redbridge to meet Kika's trainer Roz.

Kika after going head first into a badger hole in Greenwich Park. I got a few laughs on the way home as an incredibly muddy Kika was guiding me.

Home or away, Kika loves nothing more than a good splash at the beach and a roll around in the wet sand.

Since Kika came into my life, my weekends and every spare moment are spent in the park.

Diwali 2015 – our first as a family of three. I was so proud and happy to start the Hindu New Year with Kika by my side.

Rob, Mel and Desi from Guide Dogs London with me at the Neasden Temple ready to train the temple volunteers on how to guide visually impaired visitors.

August 2016 – the day Abhi was born. It had been a long night for all of us, but Kika stayed beside Seema and me throughout.

Kika is always looking out for Abhi. When he was a baby, she would often be found sleeping by the side of his Moses basket.

A day out in the Surrey Hills with a newborn Abhi and Kika.

ABOVE I was always determined to be a hands-on dad, and with Kika beside me, I'm able to be just that. LEFT On our way to Crete for a family holiday. Kika was invited into the cockpit of the plane and got to wear the captain's hat. BELOW Family time is always so special. When I lost my sight, I couldn't even imagine my future, let alone dream that we would have children and be able to travel.

I'm a firm believer that grassroots campaigning can make a difference. Delivering a petition to 10 Downing Street with Abhi and Kika.

One of my proudest campaigning moments. With my local MP Clive Efford, who I took on a blindfolded walk of the high street. We were accompanied by Emily Marr from the RNIB.

The Big Walk in 2018. One of the groups that we visited was a boxing club – of course, it would have been rude not to give it a try.

Driving the Toyota GT86, aka the 'Reasonably Fast Car' from *Top Gear*, was only ever a dream for me. With the help of my navigator Mark Watkins, it became reality.

Hosting my own Big Lunch street party in our corner of south-east London. It was an enormous success, with neighbours coming together over food and drink for the first time in years.

Kika has been by Abhi's side since the day he was born and their bond grows stronger every day.

Kika is equally protective of her new little sister and loves nothing more than a snuggle with her.

first solo trip out earlier in the year. Frustratingly, I had to stay in bed while Seema and Abhi took Kika out for walks.

Neither was the journey home quite as smooth as the journey out. Abhi had picked up a bug towards the end of the trip and, halfway through the flight, he vomited all over me! As soon as we were back home, I was admitted to hospital for another few weeks. What was supposed to be a relaxing holiday ended up in a lot of stress. It made us wonder if it had been worth the hassle.

We would have better luck, though. Exactly a year later, when Abhi was twenty months old, we took our second family holiday abroad. This time we went to Crete. We chose an all-inclusive resort, thinking it might be easier than trying to find restaurants that were happy to take Kika.

We'd made arrangements for an accessible transfer to the hotel, given that the travel agents had advised that a coach transfer would be difficult for us. However, when we arrived at the resort, we were told that they'd had to change our room. We'd been very specific about what we needed so we were wary of being put in a room that didn't meet our needs, so Seema went to check it out. When she reported back, I could tell she was full of excitement. Our new room had its own private pool! We could not have been more spoiled.

The TUI staff who looked after us in Crete were amazing. A picture of Kika and me was circulated internally so that everyone on the team would know who we were. Meanwhile, other guests at the resort were fascinated to see Kika guide me around every day and were full of questions – adults and children alike – and wanted to get to know her. In seven days, we had perhaps one meal alone as a family without having other people invite themselves to join us. That made the fact that we'd had such a generous upgrade with a private pool even more valuable. With a guide dog, you can never blend in to the crowd and I am grateful for the social media profile Kika and I have built up. But though people generally mean well when they come over to introduce themselves, sometimes I just want to switch off, as does Kika, and enjoy the quality family time.

There was one small upset on our trip to Crete which made the trip memorable. Kika has a pet passport and, under European law, if she's away from the UK for more than five days she has to take a worming tablet before she can return home. Seema arranged an appointment with a local vet prior to the holiday and the hotel staff were kind enough to drive Seema and Kika to the appointment while I looked after Abhi. It should have been straightforward, but when the vet examined Kika, he 'discovered' a fatty lump on her leg and wanted to quarantine her because of it. Now, we already knew about this lump. Our regular vet back in London had run tests and had assured us that it wasn't an issue. Fatty lumps are quite common in Labradors. After numerous phone calls to the hotel for translations and lots of animated discussion, the vet in Crete was, thankfully, eventually convinced of the same and decided that Kika should be allowed to fly home.

That hiccup in Crete didn't put us off travelling abroad with Kika. More recently, we've been to Lanzarote in the Canary Islands, where Kika and Abhi enjoyed playing on the island's famous black sand beaches. Kika has also accompanied me on business trips within Europe. She's an old hand at catching the Eurostar, whose staff are always delighted to see her.

All the same, Kika's a different dog when she's abroad – she's more cautious, slower in pace and takes a day or so to build up her confidence. In Paris, for example, this is because the traffic is suddenly coming from the other side, the tactile paving is completely different and not always consistent. There are also lots of café tables and chairs on the pavement which are difficult to get past without walking on the road. Then there are the electric scooters which can catch her off-guard. It's all different and disorienting but Kika still manages to guide me safely by concentrating hard. Then, just when she gets used to it all, we're back on the Eurostar on our way home.

But at every meeting she never fails to break the ice and win people over. At a wedding we went to in Paris last year, the guests loved her so much that she was invited onto the dance floor with them, almost rivalling the bride for their attention!

21

Changing Attitudes

Kika was easily Abhi's best friend, but we wanted to make sure he had plenty of human friends too. Before long, he was old enough to go to a local playgroup. As with everything else, I wanted to be there for this latest first in Abhi's life. I wasn't going to miss out on anything. Naturally, Kika came too.

It was great to be among other parents with young children, sharing our experiences of parenthood so far. The only problem was, everybody wanted to play with Kika. She was getting attention from everyone – kids and adults – but she was supposed to be on duty. I duly asked the other parents to keep their children from interfering with Kika, explaining that if she was distracted and moved, she would move me too, and if I was holding Abhi at the time, that could put us both in danger. The staff also tried to help explain the situation, but I could tell from their mutterings that some of the other parents at the group didn't understand and thought I was being standoffish.

I went to the playgroup a few times after that, but it was as if I was there and yet *not* there. I was always the only dad there on a weekday and if anyone did talk to me, they would strike up a conversation about Kika rather than Abhi, asking about her instead. And if Seema wasn't with me to get the conversation rolling, the other parents wouldn't interact with me at all. After a few weeks of sitting there feeling like a sore thumb, I decided not to go back to the playgroup again. I didn't need to be made to feel like an outsider. Abhi and I would go to the park instead. He loved the swings and I was able to push him on one, making sure that Kika stood so that she wouldn't be in danger of getting hit.

But the mums from the playgroup also came to the park – I could recognize their voices – and I would often hear their whispers of consternation. 'Where's *his* carer?' somebody once asked. 'How can he really be safe alone with the child? You need eyes in the back of your head to look after a toddler.' When I talked about it with Seema, she reluctantly told me about some more of the things I didn't see. Even some of the *friendly* conversations I thought I'd had with other parents were accompanied by disapproving facial expressions.

Did people really think that Abhi wasn't safe with me? Did they think that disability prevents you from being a normal parent? Sometimes it seemed to me that 'normal parents' weren't doing such a great job themselves. Once, when I was out with Kika, a child on a scooter came hurtling into me as I walked down the road. The child's mum immediately told me, 'Your dog should have got you out the way!' I could tell that the woman was at least twenty metres away when her child veered into me, but somehow she'd decided it was up to Kika to work out how to avoid him rather than her job as a mother to make sure her child wasn't out of control.

As was almost certainly the case with that particular woman, I came to understand that many people only say hurtful things to make themselves feel better when they know that they're the one who really screwed up. But, alas, some people really are just mean. Or thoughtless.

Soon Abhi was old enough to go to nursery. When I was dropping him off on my own for the first time, one of the mums said to me, 'You're really brave.' Her tone of pity really got to me. I didn't want to be considered 'brave'. I only wanted to blend in with the other parents. I had the same first day jitters as them for the same reasons. I'm no superhero. Blindness is as old as mankind and people have always adapted. That's just what I was doing.

Changing attitudes about disability is mainly about education. That's why I do my best to talk about my life and introduce Kika to the wider community wherever possible in the hope of dispelling some of the myths about guide dogs and sight loss. For every disheartening comment I've had to brush off, there have been moments when it's been truly rewarding.

The year Abhi was born, Dave Kent invited us to join him at St Christopher's Hospice. He said he'd like me to give a talk and introduce Kika to the residents, their families and carers. Dave and his guide dog Chad and his now retired guide dog Quince had been visiting the hospice – which specializes in therapy for young adults – for years. We were delighted to be invited – the staff there do so much to ensure that the hospice is a place of real joy and we knew the impact that Kika and Chad would have on the residents.

Kika was very happy to be at St Christopher's. As soon as we walked through the door, she started wagging her tail like crazy. Since I knew that everyone would want to meet her,

I let her off her lead so she could wander round saying hello and making new friends.

Just as Kika had been so kind and careful around Seema throughout her pregnancy, that day she seemed to have an instinct for where her presence would be most appreciated. After touring the room like a professional, giving everyone a moment or two of her time – Kika could have been in the royal family – she finally lay down beside a young woman in a wheelchair. The young woman's family told me that she hadn't smiled and laughed so much in a long time. Kika's company had given her a real boost. When we got home that day, Seema told me that the atmosphere was so happy and there was so much laughter that she'd forgotten we were in a hospice.

That first visit to St Christopher's, we took only Kika. A year later, in 2017, we took Abhi along too – needless to say, baby cuddles only added to the joy. From the moment Abhi was born, we wanted to make sure the public events to which Kika was invited were a family affair. Whenever Seema and I were out in central London shaking the bucket for Guide Dogs we would take Abhi along, and he proudly wore his 'my big sister is a life-changer' T-shirt to his first Guide Dogs volunteers' Christmas party. Of course Abhi would come to St Christopher's.

By our third visit, Abhi was toddling, so in order to make sure both son and dog behaved impeccably, we took Abhi and Kika to Sydenham Park for a good run around first in an attempt to tire them both out. It sort of worked.

At the hospice, Abhi was so proud to be with his 'big sis' Kika. We all gathered in a circle as Abhi took Kika's collar and walked her around, introducing her to everyone. It was even more fun than the first year. They made a great double act.

Kika has a great affinity with children and they just love her. Whenever we drop Abhi off at nursery, the other children in his class are always excited to see her. They all love to give her a tummy rub and when she's momentarily off duty, while I talk to the nursery staff, she's more than happy to oblige. It's no wonder there have been occasions when Kika hasn't wanted to leave Abhi and his little friends to get on with their day. She likes to settle herself on the floor by the children and often refuses to move. The only way to cheer her up after a nursery drop-off is by taking her to the park for a run before we go back to work.

I hope that the children Kika meets in the course of our family life and my professional engagements will all go on to share the message that visual impairment does not have to hold someone back, particularly if the wider community and the next generation recognizes the contribution of guide dogs and does its best to accommodate them without fuss. Unfortunately, the message doesn't seem to be getting through to some of the grown-ups.

22

The Kika Effect

After moving house, my schedule got busier and busier with advisory and speaking work. Suddenly, Kika and I were in and out of central London most weekdays.

Mostly, the commute went well, but as we did it more and more, there were often times when I could tell that Kika wasn't happy. Sometimes she would stop dead or try to back me into a corner to keep me safe. I started to work out some of the things that upset her: I know she dislikes the big fans that keep the Underground cool on hot days; a bottleneck at the start of an escalator can make her anxious if she struggles to find the space to step on safely; and all over the Underground there are strange echoes that must sometimes make it hard for her to hear my instructions. Other noises make it difficult too – the rumble of roller cases, squelchy shoes on a rainy day, conversations and shouting, the humming of the escalator, the rumble of the trains. Any of those noises might startle her.

One day, Kika stopped dead in her tracks between escalators for no apparent reason, walked across me and sat down by my feet, blocking my way. I could feel a flurry of people trying to race around us and could hear the next set of escalators just a few metres in front. I wasn't sure what had made

Kika stop so suddenly in such an awkward place. I felt embarrassed knowing that all eyes were on me. After a few knocks
to my shoulder and a few people stumbling over Kika, I tried
to move her.

'Kika?' I said loudly. 'Up.' But nothing.

Then I heard some heels clicking on the tiled floor behind
me. A woman ran up and asked me if I was OK before, to
my horror, revealing that she'd just seen someone take a swipe
at Kika with an umbrella.

'Was it an accident?' I asked.

'No. They did it absolutely on purpose,' the woman said.
I could hear that she was almost as shocked and angry as I
was. No wonder Kika had stopped.

When we got out of the station and found ourselves
somewhere less busy, I crouched down to talk to Kika and
reassure her. I couldn't feel any injury but she was obviously
shaken by what had happened and, now that I knew about
it, so was I.

When we got home, Seema was horrified to hear that
someone had deliberately tried to hurt Kika. She couldn't
believe that anyone would be so cruel to an animal, particularly an assistance animal.

'It must have been a one-off,' Seema said, but we both
knew we couldn't be sure. We decided we needed to know
more about Kika's experience of the commute and so we
fitted her with a camera to give us her point of view.

Just a couple of days later, as Seema and I reviewed the
footage of that day's commute, Seema spotted that a very
smartly dressed woman – on her way to work no doubt – had
swiped at Kika with her handbag. Seema cried out as she

watched the incident unfold. It happened just as we were getting on the escalator.

Kika's escalator training means she always puts me to the right of the escalator then waits for me to put my hand on the rail before stepping on at my instruction. It's a manoeuvre that needs to be done carefully. We obviously weren't fast enough for this particular woman, who expressed her annoyance with a swing of her expensive bag, hitting Kika on her back, before she carried on up the escalator without even so much as glancing over her shoulder to see how we'd reacted.

This wasn't the only negative incident by any means. By this time, I was tweeting regularly about our daily adventures, but I was in two minds about whether to put the nasty stuff out. Social media can be a minefield. Twitter can definitely go two ways. I knew that if I talked about something happening on the commute, there would be people who would immediately tell me I shouldn't be commuting at all. Or they'd want to know why Kika was on an escalator anyway. Strangely, I found that other members of the VI community could be the most judgemental of all. I'd been warned not to 'rock the boat' for those who preferred to suffer in silence.

But I believed – and still believe – it is important to get the message out. If a guide dog has lots of bad experiences such as what happened on the escalator that day, they can start to give up. I knew Kika well enough to be able to feel through the movement of the harness when she was getting despondent. She would walk more slowly with her tail down. I didn't want her to be unhappy for my sake. I could have stayed at home, only asking Kika to walk me to and from the supermarket, but on the other hand, why should I have to curtail my life because of other people's impatience and rudeness?

In the end, I decided I would put a video of someone behaving badly towards Kika out there. It was time to let people know the truth.

The video I chose was a short clip of us negotiating an escalator at another station. We were on our way to give a talk at Liverpool Street for a large corporation. I'd asked for assistance at London Bridge so Kika and I were being walked through the station by a member of staff. The staff member accompanied us onto the escalator, standing in front. As we got halfway down the escalator, I heard someone running down the metal steps behind us. It was a man.

'Could you just move?' he asked. I explained to him that because I was visually impaired and had a guide dog, I could not get out of his way. He'd have to wait just a few more seconds.

'But you're holding everyone up here,' the man told me. 'You're being inconsiderate.'

That was when the staff member accompanying us pointed out that the only inconsiderate one in this scenario was the man himself. Other commuters soon got involved, taking my side.

The irony is, that even though the rude man was supposed to be in such a hurry, on reviewing Kika's camera footage, it seems we easily overtook him later on.

I posted the video on Kika's Twitter feed with a polite caption that I hoped would allow the viewer to make up their own mind about the situation. It read, 'If you see a #GuideDog

on an escalator please wait patiently behind. Under no circumstances should you try to push through! I'm trained to
hold my ground and keep Dad and myself safe. Great job
by @TfL staff who was with us.'

The reaction was immediate. I had expected a response
from the visually impaired community, but the tweet also
garnered huge support from the general public. Ninety-nine
per cent of the messages I received were positive. People were
outraged that someone would be so rude and entitled that
they'd think they had priority over a guide dog owner. The
clip started trending on social media and went viral. Soon it
had 10,400 retweets and 17,100 likes, over two million impres-
sions and 507,000 media views. All this from Kika's relatively
small Twitter following. Then the traditional press picked up
the story.

The incident was covered in the media in Korea, Canada,
Australia and the States. In the UK, I talked to the BBC and
Sky. I was stunned by the interest our story had stirred up
worldwide. The news even got as far as my grandmother in
Madhya Pradesh. She read all about it in the *Times of India*!

I wasn't at all prepared for the attention that single clip
gathered but I knew I had to make the most of it. I also knew
I had to make sure I didn't get a reputation as 'angry Amit'
(whenever I write a tweet that could be construed as angry,
I do get Seema to give it a sanity check). I couldn't just rant
about how selfish some people were. I had to turn our suddenly expanded media profile into an opportunity to highlight the problems associated with sight loss and educate
people as to how they might help a visually impaired person.

I'm often asked why I'm so outspoken, why I campaign

on accessibility issues and why I talk about them on social media. Of course, what you see on social media is only a fraction of our daily lives. If I posted every negative interaction and experience, it would make it a very unhappy feed indeed, but my aim has always been to push for change, so that the next person to come along doesn't have to go through what I did. It would be much easier for me to just post cute pictures of Kika or not bother at all, given that writing a tweet using dictation is no mean feat. But it's important that I keep campaigning and not just for my own sake.

It is tiring and working through the negativity takes its toll, but I've seen incredibly positive and practical changes as a result of my active engagement. 2018 was a particularly big year in that regard. After that escalator video and the attention it gathered, I became involved with Transport for All, a campaign to ensure better transport experiences for the elderly and disabled.

Then, when I won Transport for All's 'Make A Noise' award for my efforts to get the accessibility message out on social media, Transport for London asked if I could do something for them. The result was that Kika and I fronted TfL's priority seating campaign. I recorded audio announcements that were played out in stations across London. Of course, Kika was with me when I made the recordings and is in every photo. The announcement said, 'Hello, my name is Amit Patel and I'm supporting Priority Seating Week. If you see someone wearing a Baby on Board or Please Offer Me a Seat badge, please offer yours if you can.'

I also attended a TfL area managers' meeting to discuss how we could raise awareness of the problem and other related issues. I was able to highlight the good experiences I'd had when travelling through London and recognize the positive impact of proper staff training in assisting disabled passengers. However, I also flagged where more needed to be done in terms of ensuring that assistance was always available when needed.

I often rely on railway staff to help me on my commute and, most of the time, the staff Kika guides me to are very helpful. But not always. On occasion, when I've asked which platform my train will be leaving from, they've said 'Isn't it obvious?' before realizing that the reason I have a guide dog is because I can't see.

Once I happened to be at London Bridge station at the same time as a VIP – not another visually impaired person in this case, but a 'very important' one. It was Prince William, second in line to the throne.

When we arrived at the station, Kika followed the crowd in the usual direction, but the route we normally took was closed off. When I realized what was going on, I asked Kika to find a staff member to help us find another way through. Kika did as I instructed, identifying them by their jackets. Standing in front of the staff members, I asked for help. No one responded. At least, not to me. I could hear them having a conversation among themselves about who should deal with me. None of them wanted to move from the prime spot they were standing in because they all wanted to see Prince William.

I asked for help again. Louder this time. Still they ignored me. I asked one more time and finally one of the staff members acknowledged me. 'I didn't see you there,' he said.

Reviewing the footage from Kika's camera that evening,

Seema confirmed that, just as I suspected, the staff were taking the mick. They had seen me. They'd looked right at me. They'd talked about me loudly enough for me to hear.

We posted about the incident on Twitter and social media erupted once again. No one could believe the arrogance of those station staff members. It was disheartening to say the least, but it gave me another opportunity to show people just how hard it can be to navigate the world with a visual impairment. Thankfully, most people, when they understand the problem, are only too pleased to do what they can.

The London Bridge incident was picked up by the BBC. Asad Ahmed from BBC London News came to our house to interview me about it. For the filming, I was holding Abhi, who was only five months old at this point. As they counted down to going live on BBC London evening news, I thought that Abhi felt a little warm, but didn't quite register why. When the interview finished, Asad wanted to take some photos with us before the team left, but Seema was absolutely insistent that she needed to whisk Abhi away. While I'd been holding him, Abhi had done an enormous poo that had gone all the way up his back and leaked through his clothes. I obviously couldn't see it but Abhi was covered, though he was very much enjoying himself, judging by his huge smiles throughout the interview. Asad got his photo but those clothes never quite recovered!

Around the same time, I added my voice to the protest against the concept of 'shared space'. You've probably got some 'shared space' in a town near you. It refers to a space where cars, pedestrians and cyclists all share the same thoroughfare with no physical demarcation between the road and the pavement. They're all on the same level. There are no road markings and no kerbs. The idea is that shared space makes a more pleasant environment for socializing and shopping. The lack of markings is supposed to encourage drivers and cyclists to slow down and pay more attention to pedestrians. The reality is far from that utopia. Shared space might look good in a town planner's mock-up of a modern urban centre, but in practice it's a nightmare. The drivers act as though they have priority. Meanwhile pedestrians don't have any means of crossing safely as they would do with normal pavements and button-operated pedestrian crossings. For a guide dog owner, whose dog has been trained to navigate the urban landscape kerb to kerb, no kerbs mean that the dog is at a loss for where to go and a shared space becomes essentially a no-go place.

I'd experienced the problems myself. On one occasion, I went up to Preston by train. Seema was already there with Abhi, visiting her parents. The plan was that she would pick Kika and me up from the station but she got held up and rather than sit in the draughty station, I thought it would be a good idea to get some coffee and let Kika stretch her legs.

I remembered from previous visits that the high street was only a few minutes' walk from the railway station so decided to venture out. I noticed immediately that Kika was a little hesitant as we walked, but put it down to her having had a good snooze on the train up. However, her pace was slow and she seemed unsure of where to go, despite my clear commands. We made it onto the high street and then I asked Kika to find the kerb, knowing that Brucciani's, the coffee shop that Seema had taken me to previously, was just across the road. Having been in there a few times before, I hoped Kika would recognize it. However the command was lost on her completely. Kika stood still. I could hear buses coming down the road so I knew that we were in the right place. I tried the command 'find the crossing' which prompts Kika to take me to a pelican or zebra crossing but still nothing. Kika still wasn't moving. By this point, I started wondering if I wasn't quite where I thought I was. So I called Seema and explained what had happened and what route I had taken. She was soon by my side. As soon as Seema arrived, she knew exactly what had happened.

Since our last visit there, Preston city centre had become a shared space zone, which meant there was no longer a raised kerb separating the pavement from the road. Taxis were stopped on the side, buses were coming past and people were walking down the middle. As guide dogs are trained to go from kerb to kerb, this meant Kika was lost – the changed layout confused her.

As the fashion for shared spaces in town centres continues – and especially since the new electric cars are all but impossible to hear coming – the visually impaired, the disabled, the elderly and people with small children are increasingly going to out-of-town retail parks where they can feel safer. Far from making town centres the place to be, shared space is killing them off.

You can probably tell that shared space is something I feel very strongly about. Kika and I took the protest against it to Westminster. Abhi came with us – he was a little over a year old at the time – when we knocked on the door of 10 Downing Street to hand in a petition.

A petition is great, but most of the time the message still doesn't get to the relevant people. I knew that as well as gathering signatures, I needed to make personal connections to make my message stick. So I engaged my MP, Clive Efford, on a local shared space scheme that I struggled to navigate. Fortunately, he was quick to understand and come on side, meeting with me to discuss the issues, accompanying me to Downing Street to hand in yet more petitions, and attending various charity-led guide dog access events.

At the end of 2018, I was awarded a Points of Light Award by the prime minister for all the campaigning I'd done so far. These awards are given to outstanding individuals – people who are making a change in their community.

The award came as a massive, but very welcome, surprise. There's no way I would have even dreamed of being recognized like this back when I first lost my sight and I was barely able to step out of the house alone. It was lovely for all the work and effort that I'd put in to be recognized, though the driver for me remains the fact that I can deliver real change which has an impact for real people.

When he read about the award, Clive sent me a tweet asking, 'How about that blindfold walk you promised me?'

Working with the RNIB, I arranged to take Clive and his team along my local high street so they could experience it as I do. I wanted Clive to walk the length of it with a white cane. The moment he put a mind fold on and stepped out on his own with the cane, he was petrified. Though he knew the neighbourhood well, he soon discovered that when the lights are out and you're reliant on the white cane and your hearing, it's a whole different world.

As we took Clive along the street, he noted the lack of kerbs and discovered that the benches on the footpath had very sharp corners. But I think it really hit him when he got into the 'shared space'. Clive was walking along happily with his white cane, then he bumped into a parked van. He kept bumping into the van, seemingly unable to get around it. As he was doing this, another car pulled up right behind him. All the time Clive kept telling me that cars don't park in shared spaces and that drivers should know better. He was discovering the reality of that theory.

When we got back to his office, he asked me, 'Do you think we should have a meeting with the town planners about that courtesy crossing?' Clive knew that a courtesy crossing – one with no buttons or light, which relies on the pedestrian making eye contact with the driver – had been earmarked for the high street. Now he understood much more clearly why a crossing like that would not work for someone like me.

Clive took up the fight and he soon got us a meeting with the town planners. I pulled in Hugh Huddy and Emily Marr from the RNIB's policy and parliamentary team to help make the case for how difficult a courtesy crossing is when you can't see. I was so proud when I heard that it had been pulled at the last minute, in favour of finding a better solution. It was a major result and the perfect example of how individuals can drive change and make an impact.

It isn't all glamorous meetings in Westminster, however; I spend a lot of time doing grassroots campaigning on the phone as well as sending emails and letters about the issues I feel need addressing – from the dangerously sharp edges on lift button panels (where I cut my hand on multiple occasions) to training railway staff on how to safely guide a visually impaired person. Often I don't hear back for months, but this regular engagement has led to more and more organizations approaching me directly to work with them to improve their services.

As well as taking Clive Efford on that blindfolded walk, I was invited by Nus Ghani MP, then Undersecretary of State for Transport, alongside representatives from the Department for Transport, Network Rail and Southeastern trains to take a journey with her to highlight how challenging train travel is when you're blind. I wanted to showcase that it's made even more challenging when the infrastructure isn't designed to support us.

Showing Ghani and the others how I navigate an unfamiliar station with Kika on one side and a buggy or small child on the other, when there are no lifts available and no staff members on the platform to assist me, helped to bring home to them how much improvement to access and infrastructure around stations is needed. On the train journey we took that day, the audio announcements were for a different line to the one we were actually on. Everyone was confused, but at least the others could look out of the window to see where we were. I can't.

I'm pretty confident now. I'll go out regardless and will always find someone to help me, but not everyone in my position feels so self-assured or able to ask for the help they need. It's easy for one negative experience to put you off going out at all. Especially when it feels like the whole world was designed against you. Taking Nus Ghani and those senior transport execs around gave them a graphic illustration of the importance of having sufficient, easily identifiable and well-trained staff on stations. It showed them that it is vital to make sure that audio station announcements on trains are kept on – even at night – so a blind person always knows what station they are at. It showed the need for the physical infrastructure to be correct too, such as having tactile paving running along the edge of the platform so a white cane user is able to keep away from the edge and stay safe. I know the journey gave all my companions food for thought.

It's also important to me that visually impaired people feel properly included in their communities. I got a chance to work on that when Kika and I met Lindsey Brummitt, programme director at The Eden Project Communities, the famous Cornish conservation centre's community arm. She told me all about The Big Walk, which was to start in Morecambe that year. It's designed to shine a light on the people at the heart of the UK's communities, who work together to make great things happen. It culminates in The Big Lunch, which is a series of street parties to promote community cohesion. In 2018, TV chef Ainsley Harriott was one the celebrities supporting the initiative. I was familiar with Ainsley not only from watching *Ready Steady Cook* when I was younger but also from hearing his voice on the CBeebies show *My World Kitchen*, which is one of Abhi's favourites. When Ainsley met Kika, he sang to her. She was instantly enchanted and Ainsley had a friend for life.

Lindsey thought Kika and I would be the perfect addition to the walking team, given all of my campaigning work and interest in the project. Naturally, Kika was always going to be up for a big walk! We agreed to join the Eden Project team, starting in Nottingham, and stopping at various community projects on our way home to London.

Kika and I were part of a team of four. Our Big Walk started with a morning's hike to a council estate in Nottingham city centre, where the locals had set up a community garden. We met so many great people who had dedicated their time to tending the garden as a way to bring the local community together. They ran activities centred around gardening including short courses on growing your own produce as well as family activity days. We had lunch there. An eighty-something woman who had lived on the estate for most of her life told us that meeting Kika had brightened up her day.

It was a fantastic start, but the next part of the walk, from Nottingham to Birmingham, was terrible. It took place over a couple of days. We were covering around twenty kilometres a day, mostly off-road. It was by far the most physical thing I'd done since losing my sight. It was also a big deal for me to be away from Seema for so long and staying in a different place every night. And it poured with rain all the way. By the time we got to the next official stop, at a boxing club in Birmingham, Kika and I were wet through. I could feel through the harness that Kika was not too happy about that.

Meeting the people at the boxing club perked us up, though. The organizers had set the club up to provide local kids with something to do that would keep them off the streets. They were having great success by persuading the kids to channel their energy into sport rather than into gangs and crime.

Our final day of the 2018 Big Walk ended in Hackney,

east London. To Kika's delight, her new friend Ainsley was there for The Big Lunch along with fellow supporter Jo Brand. After all that walking, we deserved a *very* big lunch. It was a real celebration that made all those long miles in the pouring rain worth the effort. And before I knew it, I'd agreed to host a Big Lunch of my own the following year.

23

The Girl in the White Dress

'Let's give a warm welcome to Dr Amit Patel . . .'

As Kika walked me onto the stage in front of an audience of two hundred corporate lawyers, I was confident that the afternoon would go well. I'd taken great care to prepare my speech on how the company I was addressing could improve accessibility at its London head office. I had my braille notes in my hand. Once safely on stage, I dropped Kika's harness and she settled down on the floor nearby as my host helped me navigate the last few steps to the lectern and showed me how to adjust the microphone. I had already had a guided tour of the venue earlier in the day. I knew roughly how big it was, how the chairs were laid out and where the doors were.

I've developed a strategy for public speaking in any venue I didn't know as a sighted person. In my mind's eye, I super-impose the characteristics of a venue I remember from the time before I went blind. Sometimes it's my junior school assembly hall. Sometimes it's the lecture theatre from medical school. Imagining myself somewhere I know well helps me to feel calm and centred before I begin to talk. On this particular occasion, I imagined myself back at junior school with its wooden floors, rows of benches and gym equipment hanging from the walls. I could almost smell the distinctive floor polish.

Fixing my gaze on a spot at the back of the room – right where the doors would have been in that old assembly hall – I cleared my throat and began my speech. I ran my finger across my braille notes and spoke fluently, throwing in the occasional ad-libbed joke. My audience chuckled along with me. I was soon confident that I had them on side. From somewhere behind me, I could hear Kika's distinctive snore.

'You can tell she's heard this speech before . . .' I quipped. A wave of laughter lifted the room. I had the audience in the palm of my hand. But then I saw her.

At first I told myself I could just ignore her.

'And as I was saying . . .' I tried to continue my speech. But soon my finger seemed frozen on the braille dots in front of me. My voice dried up in my throat. She wasn't going away. She was getting closer, floating down the middle of my junior school assembly hall with her black eyes fixed firmly on mine.

'. . . as I was saying . . .'

Her long dark hair drifted around her head like seaweed on the tide. Her simple cotton dress was ripped and dirty. Tears of blood dripped down her bone-white face. She was getting so close I could have reached out and touched her. She opened her mouth as if to say something. As if to scream.

I grasped the edges of the lectern as I felt my knees grow weak in her presence. My braille notes scattered on the floor . . .

There is still much work to be done to teach the general public about sight loss. Some of its consequences and challenges are obvious, but I had no idea about certain things until they happened to me. Take Charles Bonnet Syndrome.

Charles Bonnet Syndrome (CBS) occurs in people who once had sight but later lost it. It doesn't affect those who have been visually impaired from birth. It causes hallucinations that are almost always unpleasant and disturbing. Sufferers see snakes and worms, miniature people and goblins, to name but a few of the syndrome's many and varied horrors. They seem to embody the very things you're really afraid of.

Charles Bonnet first observed the syndrome in the 1760s while taking care of his grandfather, who went blind in old age. Until recently, few people were aware of the syndrome, so it was originally attributed to a psychological rather than physical condition. That's understandable. I know that when I started getting my own hallucinations, I thought I was going mad.

Looking back, I've worked out that the first time I experienced CBS was after I'd had a corneal transplant. I thought I saw someone leaning over my bed as I lay there recovering from my operation. The vision was incredibly vivid. After that I would often see people or things that weren't really there.

My CBS hallucinations now take the same form every time and, unfortunately for me, that form is a vision of the girl from *The Ring*. Have you ever seen *The Ring*? It's a horror film – a remake of a Japanese classic – in which a group of teenagers get hold of a cursed videotape. Legend has it that anyone who watches the footage on the tape dies within seven days. The villain of the piece is a vengeful ghost called Samara, who was murdered by being thrown down a well. The videotape shows her climbing out of the well where she met her death. She is dressed all in white, with her dark hair shrouding her face like a horrible veil. When you do get to see her eyes through her hair, they are evil.

Yep. That's what I hallucinate several times a day, every day: an evil ghost. As an extra touch, sometimes my Samara has blood pouring from her eyes as she floats through empty space towards me. Sometimes she's just crawled out of her grave and she's covered in mud. The very worst of it is that she can appear at any moment: when I'm having my breakfast, when I'm walking down the street, when I'm climbing up the stairs – I once fell down the stairs thanks to a sudden appearance – or when I'm sitting at my desk. She's even appeared when I've been changing Abhi. She doesn't care whether I'm at home or at work. The time she materialized when I was on stage, which I've just described, was a particularly tough moment. She never gets any less horrifying but at least I now understand how she's triggered.

Though I'm technically blind, there is one tiny clear pixel in my vision, in the upper right-hand corner of my right eye. When that pixel lets in light, my brain tries frantically to interpret what it means. So, say I'm walking to the train station and a white van races by. That flash of white caught by the last working cell in my retina can cause Samara to appear. As can a train tearing through a station while I'm standing still on the platform, or the landscape going by while I'm actually on a train. Samara appears on nearly every commute.

How do I get rid of her? If I'm on my own, I always listen to music to distract me. If that doesn't work, I wave my arms in front of my face until she disappears, or I shout and tell her to go away, but of course there are situations – such as on the commute or at a presentation – when I don't want to be telling an invisible ghost girl to bugger off.

When I was walking with a white cane and a hallucination happened, I would start sweating, feel angry and have to stop until the moment passed. Since I've had Kika in my life, it's been better. Kika is very good at telling when I've got ghostly company. Sometimes she seems to know before I've even registered what's going on. If we're on the train and I can't physically push the ghost away without worrying other passengers, then Kika will rest her head on my knee and breathe heavily to remind me that I'm not alone. Hearing her breathing deeply reminds me to do the same. On that day when Samara appeared while I was addressing the auditorium full of lawyers, Kika came to the rescue, calmly padding over and resting her head against my leg and staying there until the ghost was gone and I was ready to continue.

Before I lost my sight, I didn't know much about CBS despite my medical training. Even people working in the eye profession who know about CBS may never have encountered anyone with it and thus don't have an understanding of how it can affect someone in their day-to-day life. People are always shocked when I tell them about my hallucinations. I can understand why people might think someone with CBS is just going crazy.

Over the past couple of years, it has become more widely known thanks to people such as journalist and campaigner Judith Potts, who first came to know about it when it affected her own mother. After seeing her go through terrible fear and anguish, Potts was moved to set up Esme's Umbrella, a charity to raise awareness of the syndrome. In 2017, she was behind the first ever Charles Bonnet Syndrome Awareness Day. In 2018, Moorfields Eye Hospital had their own awareness event at which I was a key speaker.

I also attended a Vision Strategy UK meeting about funding research into why the hallucinations happen. The RNIB estimates that some half a million visually impaired people are affected. There may be many more. So far it's not been adequately recorded. Can you imagine any other disorder that affects so many people going unexplored?

I've always tried to be brutally honest about how the syndrome affects me. If by campaigning for awareness I can save even a single person from having to go through the awful experience of wondering if they've gone mad as well as blind, it'll be worth it.

24

Seema's Story

I remember just lying there, curled up in a ball on the bed of the spare room. I had the curtains drawn so that it was dark. The only faint light was from the phone in my hand. And I was crying. Not just crying, but sobbing.

Only a year and a half earlier I had married the man of my dreams (well, almost – he was a vegetarian at this point, after all) after a whirlwind cross-Channel romance and a big, colourful Indian wedding. We took our vows in front of hundreds of people on a day filled with joy and hope for the future. We'd made plans: to travel the world together, decorate the house (mainly me), grow vegetables (mainly him) and to have children eventually – a boy and a girl. We'd even chosen names. I wanted a boy first, him a girl. It was nothing out of the ordinary – just normal, happy married life.

Then overnight Amit lost his sight.

My hopes, dreams and plans for the future were in shreds. The man that I had fallen so madly in love with, who had somehow reached so deeply into my soul and hooked me in, had disappeared. In his place sat a shadow of the man that I married.

A man that right now was barely even talking to me. We were like strangers, hardly communicating. Even a gentle hand on his shoulder would be brushed off with 'I'm fine, leave me alone.' He was pushing me away and I knew it.

I can't remember how long this went on for; it felt like a lifetime, but it was probably only a matter of weeks. I didn't know what was going through his head at that point, but the question for me was, how did we get here? And what happened to my Amit? It broke my heart. I was so lost, all I could do was cry. This was life-changing for both of us. I was always in it for the long run, but it's old age when you expect 'complications' and health issues, not eighteen months in.

Was our life over? Our marriage? He didn't even want to speak to me. How could we possibly move forward from here? And I was angry. So angry. Why me? Why us? What had we done to deserve this? Was this my fate? Was I destined to have to look after him for the rest of my life? It just wasn't fair.

The worst thing was how alone I felt. I couldn't tell anyone about it just yet – not my family as I didn't want to worry them, and not work as I was under a lot of pressure to deliver and desperately trying to hold it together. Heaven forbid what impact any knowledge of this would have had on my career progression prospects. I was at risk of work being taken away from me as a way to 'make things easier' for me at a time when I was desperate to prove myself and get a promotion. Plus I was the sole earner now and we needed my job to survive.

Only later would I really realize the impact all of these pressures had on me. Even most of my friends couldn't understand the enormity of what we were going through and the strain it put on our relationship. There were only two people in the world – my closest friends, Celina and Krupa – who knew the truth from the off and remained my rocks through the worst of this storm.

They were the ones I was messaging in that lonely, dark room. Through the tears, their words gave me the strength to get through each day as it came, to stay strong for Amit and to continue to believe in us. And that's how I got through – one day at a time.

Deep inside, though, I always knew things would get better. I knew right from the very first day that I met Amit that he was destined for amazing things. I was the plain Jane – a sensible, quiet, stick-to-the-rules kind of girl. Amit was the confident, outspoken, energetic, impulsive, creative type. Most of all, he was a doer and he made things happen. The day that Amit was officially certified as severely sight impaired, those roles switched. I knew that if we were going to get through this and make it out to a better place, I would need to be the one to make it happen now. So I cried. And I ate, a lot. It helped at the time. Stress was doing funny things to me. Sometimes food calmed me but other times I'd have a severe panic attack on the way home from the station. But at the same time, I started to plan, think and research. I liked to think I was good at my job because I was a planner and a people person – I could change hearts and minds in the office and I made things happen there. It was time to apply that approach to my personal life. My brain was in overdrive and trying to work out a way out of the darkness was all-consuming for me.

After taking an initial week or so off to look after Amit, I went back to the office, putting on a brave face and not really telling anyone what had happened. I threw myself into work, mainly for the distraction – it helped so much to focus on something other than what was going on at home. The routine, the colleagues, the change of scene and the deadlines all helped me to take my mind off our problems. But on the train and every spare moment I got, I was working on my plan. It wasn't big or clever, but for me it was a way of getting through the day-to-day difficulties at home and hopefully moving towards something more positive. I broke it down into three steps:

Step one: stay positive with Amit. Keep engaging and talking to him. Even if he didn't acknowledge me or respond, it didn't matter how soul-destroying I found it. I had to keep trying. I knew the meds weren't helping and that he was out of it most of the time. But he needed to be reminded that I was there for him and that I loved him. And he couldn't not talk to me forever, surely . . .

Step two: work out how to get Amit some help and support. This was the real biggie as I was completely new to sight loss and everything that came with it. I mean, I'd barely stepped into a hospital in my life other than to have a routine blood test. I didn't know how to handle a long-term health condition. I also didn't know where to start in terms of accessing support services and finding someone for him to talk to. This was before we even looked at helping Amit to adapt to his sight loss in a more practical way. I had no idea who to turn to.

Step three: find a way to be around more for Amit and be closer. The commute from Guildford into central London every day was a killer, especially when the trains were delayed. I negotiated with work to work from home one day per week so that I could be around him. But that didn't help for the other four days.

It was one specific incident that triggered the idea to make a bigger change. I'd normally call Amit multiple times in a day while he was on his own at home, even if all I got was a one-word answer. I'd call when I got into London, every tea break, at lunch time, as I was leaving the office, when I was at the station and with my ETA when I was on the train home. If he ever didn't answer the phone, I knew something was wrong and, of course, rightly or wrongly, I panicked.

One day, he didn't answer the phone when I rang. Then a few more times. I panicked, explained the situation to my manager, took my laptop and ran to take the first train home to check on him. My heart was racing at a million miles an hour. I was so on edge I only imagined the worst.

When I got home, I found Amit on the sofa with cuts on his hands, which were bleeding. He'd tried to make tea but had dropped the cup full of boiling water, tried to clean it up but cut himself in the process. He'd also misplaced his phone. It took me almost two hours to get home to him that day. That had to change. I couldn't be so far away any more. Just in case.

I looked at the figures. We were on a single salary now so it was going to be tight. I started looking at flats in London online to get a feel for if a move might be possible. If we could relocate to London, it felt like it could be the answer to all of our problems. We both needed a fresh start and a flat with no stairs meant no worries about Amit falling. I wanted somewhere close to the office, close to City Airport so I could fly in and out easily for work and, more importantly, on public transport so that when Amit was ready, he could get out without being dependent on me. But all of that still felt far in the future.

Slowly, however, things did improve – he began talking more, engaging more . . . It started with little things, like accepting a cup of tea, telling me what he fancied eating for dinner, asking me if I was OK, how work was going. During those early days, every word he uttered to me gave me a spring in my step. It was when he started asking questions that I knew things were on the up and that only motivated me more. My plan was working.

A few months after that terrible day, I had to travel to New York for work. It was a trip I was dreading. I was broken by this point – no sleep, constant worry, plus work pressure. Most people would probably have handed it over to someone else, given the circumstances, but the harder things were at home, the harder I worked. It gave me great comfort to focus on something, manage the process and deliver it. Perhaps it was the feeling of making progress or getting a positive outcome, delivering something tangible, something real.

As it turned out, going through with my work trip to New York was the best thing I could have done. The freezing winter temperatures and distance from home gave me the headspace to refocus and regain some energy. A few friends also happened to be out in New York while I was there, and seeing them was the perfect remedy to take my mind off everything. Amit's parents were with him so I knew he was in safe hands. For those few days, in minus twenty-two degrees, I worked, I saw friends, I laughed for the first time in goodness knows how long and, somewhere along the way, I remembered who I was again.

Every time I went to New York for work, I did a quick whizz around Macy's, mainly for the novelty of it and also because I love shoes and handbags. I had the same routine each time: as soon as my last meeting finished, and before I had to rush back to the hotel, grab my bag and jump in a cab to the airport, I'd head to Macy's. I'd go in, take a left, head up to the visitor centre, show my passport to get my tax-free shopping card and then fast track around the hand-bags before making my way upstairs to the shoes.

This time my friends came along with me and convinced me to try out some new makeup. It was a treat to indulge myself given the weeks of worry that had just passed. I got new lipsticks, blusher, eyeshadows – I felt like a new woman. Quite the contrast to the haggard, tear-stained, dark-eyed woman I had become back at home. Another part of my New York routine was to swing by a drugstore to stock up on American sweets for Amit. Yes, I confess, my husband, a grown man, was (and still is) a stickler for sugary sweets. I piled up a few bags of Starburst jelly beans and some liquorice for good measure, along with anything else new and different I thought he might like, in the hope that such a silly gift might bring a smile to his face when I got home. True to form, the jelly beans got a little smile out of him and I saw a glimpse of the old Amit again.

Home from New York with a fresh energy and vision, I watched as Amit very slowly started to re-engage with me. He was coming to terms a bit more with his sight loss. I started to see a chink of light at the end of that tunnel. But I was so worried about pushing him in any direction that I very much left it to him to set the pace as to what he wanted to do and when.

We started small. Talking. Conversing in more than just trivial dialogue. And this opened up conversations about getting more help and support, with a view to getting him out and about again and being more independent.

I can't tell you at what point it all changed, whether it was overnight or if it was a slower and more incremental process, but at some point something clicked and Amit was talking to people, getting help and support and even considering the idea of a move to London. Of course, I was still incredibly anxious every time I left him to go to work, but I started to see a glimmer of the man I married again. And that was enough to give me all the strength I needed to carry us forward.

When Amit and I first discussed the idea of him applying for a guide dog, it was all very theoretical, but I loved the idea of having a dog. We were told the waiting list in London was at least two and a half years, so we thought we had a long time to get used to the idea, and it gave us some time to make other changes in our life, such as moving house.

As it had been a long time since I'd spent any time around dogs, volunteering for the Guide Dogs for the Blind Association seemed like a sensible thing to do. It wasn't only the dogs I was interested in. I also wanted to learn about the impact they had on their owner and family, how they guided their owner and also what day-to-day life with a guide dog around was like. The irony is, by the time I had finished my training sessions and my DBS check came back, it was too late for me to take up my volunteer role as dog exerciser – guiding VIPs around the park as their dogs had a well-earned break and playtime off the harness (or what is known in guide dog parlance as a 'free run') – on the weekends.

Because then Kika came into our lives. She may not have taken to me straight away, but I was determined to make her love me. Kika was life-changing, not just for Amit but for me too. And most definitely for our marriage. She took the pressure off me and for that I am eternally grateful to her. I know that she'll keep Amit safe when they're out together. There's no more panicking when he misses a train or thinks he's lost. It means he's more confident going out alone and able to do things independently which in turn means I don't always have to be there for everything. It was freeing for me. The first time I could ask him to pop to the shops to pick up more than milk was the best feeling for us both.

Life pre-Kika was hectic enough – of our own making, of course, with all of our changes happening in quick succession – but with her arrival we were catapulted into a whole new world and we threw ourselves into it. Volunteering for Guide Dogs took up a lot of our free time. After Abhi was born, he joined us at the various events where Amit was speaking or even when we were bucket-shaking at the supermarket. It really became a family affair, particularly while I was on maternity leave. I must admit, I loved it – it was a great feeling

239

to be giving back to the charity that had supported us so much. Plus, Amit is a brilliant speaker and he always has the audience, and me, captivated. What I really loved, however, was the feeling of how far we had come and the fact that I had my Amit back – strong, confident and happy.

Kika and Amit's public profile kept growing through social media and I suddenly found myself acting as Amit's agent and PA simultaneously, managing his diary for interviews, taking calls with journalists and briefing him in between. All while still juggling a small baby. It was busy but very fun at the time, and a great opportunity to use their platform to raise awareness of the challenges that they faced when travelling. I hoped it would change other people's behaviours in a positive way. The irony was that we never went looking for media coverage and never approached anyone with stories – everyone just came to us. Unfortunately, that meant that we also saw the really ugly side of the online world.

After Amit's escalator video spread across social media and was featured in the tabloid press, we were met with so much trolling that by spring 2018 we wanted out. Every time something from Twitter went viral, negative comments flooded in alongside the supportive ones. The web of jealousy that we were pulled into had nasty, racist undertones. Of course, they had no idea (or didn't care) about the engagement and positive work that Amit and I were doing outside of all that media attention. We were reaching out to people who weren't part of the VI community, those who had no experience of sight loss, and they were learning all about it with us through Kika's Twitter feed.

It all got too much for me. I was in tears at some of the vile comments we were receiving and I didn't even dare share most of this with Amit because I knew how much it would hurt him as well. We considered stopping it all, deleting the social media accounts and forgetting all about it. Luckily the good outweighed the bad. We'd built such a strong online community and so many people within it helped to restore our faith in humanity. And I've developed a much thicker skin as a result too.

One of the incredible things to come out of that negative experience was an invitation to visit the Calvert Trust in Exmoor. The Calvert Trust is a residential centre for outdoor activities, all of which are fully accessible, meaning they are suitable for anyone with any kind of disability. Reading about what had happened to Amit on the escalators, they wanted to do something nice for him, so I drove the family five hours down to Devon for a long weekend. It was genuinely the most fun we've had as a family in a long time – we were able to rock climb, kayak, zip-line, cycle, and all in the most beautiful setting around Wistlandpound Reservoir. If you'd told me five years ago that Amit would be scaling an outdoor climbing wall, or abseiling or kayaking, there's no way I would have believed you. But there he was, in his element. And I got to do it too. We made some beautiful family memories that weekend in Devon, all thanks to the thought-fulness of strangers.

When Kika first joined our family, I changed jobs, taking on a domestic policy role at work so that I could be more local – no more travel abroad and leaving Amit and Kika for days at a time. I'd put all of my career plans on hold over the past few years, but was feeling confident enough in our family and set-up to be able to take on more challenges and be more open about what I needed from work post Abhi's arrival too. With Abhi in nursery a few days per week and Amit looking after him for the rest, I could concentrate on myself again. After five years of putting my needs and my aspirations on the backburner, I was finally able to focus without guilt on developing myself and my career again. And my god did that feel good.

We might have hit a few roadblocks along our journey and had bad luck, but we have always been determined not to let this define us. The thing is, both Amit and I are incredibly goal-oriented, but each of us just approaches it in a different way. When we're on the same page, however, there's no stopping us and we can make things happen very quickly. Once we had decided to move to London, to get the support Amit needed and find ways to build his confidence again, things started to slot into place. We had a little helping hand from Lady Luck on the way which allowed us to upgrade from a flat in London to a house in the suburbs in just eighteen months and we met some incredible people along the way who supported us through the difficult times. Seeing our efforts come to fruition drove us even further.

Through a combination of teamwork, sheer stubbornness and hard work we've got through all of the challenges we've faced and it's made us stronger than ever.

But there are things I wish I had done differently. I'd never been through anything traumatic or needed to support someone through something so difficult before, so I was at

a loss for what to do or where to start. I certainly should
have taken some more time for myself when Amit first lost
his sight.

As the partner, it's easy to be overlooked and to put yourself second when someone you love is going through
something difficult. But the old saying is true: you can't pour
from an empty cup. Self-care takes many forms. I thought
I'd book into a spa hotel for a night with some girlfriends
when things calmed down, or take a nice bubble bath at
home. Of course, those things never happened. In truth, for
me self-care was much simpler – cooking myself something
I actually wanted to eat, or taking a walk just for the purpose
of stretching my legs and clearing my head, not to run errands.

The strain I was under eventually manifested itself as vitiligo. The funny thing about the condition is that it comes on
when you're recovering, when things are getting better. So
when I spotted a white patch on my thumb while Amit and
I were in India, over a year and a half after Amit lost his
sight, I thought nothing of it. But it didn't go away. And
gradually I got more and more patches popping up on my
hands and then my face. I was devastated. There was no
proven treatment and I was told that, once lost, the pigment
on my hands especially would be unlikely to come back. But
what was clear was that the last few years had taken their
toll on me too and it was starting to show just how heavy
that was. I'd had to be tough and carry on. I didn't know
any other way.

If anyone ever asked me how I was, I'd say I was fine,
because I genuinely thought I was coping. But I'd become
responsible for everything – financially and domestically. All

the life admin was on me and as a result I didn't have evenings free any more so 'me time' was off the agenda. My weekends were spent out with Amit as, given he was alone the whole week in the early days, I felt guilty denying him that time outside. It's no wonder I was permanently exhausted and stressed.

Stubborn me had declined any kind of assistance, insisting that I was just fine when I really should have just accepted the help. I thought I was being strong. It's only now that I've recognized that being strong takes so many forms and that there is more strength in admitting you need help and accepting it rather than denying it. All you really want when you're going through a tough time is to be normal and for people to treat you as normally as possible.

If you recognize any of the above, either in yourself or in someone close to you who is struggling to support someone else, all I can advise is to be there for them. Offer to help, take them out, take their mind off things. You don't need to fix things or make things better, because most times that's just not possible. But you can be their rock through it all, just by being there. If you yourself are the one helping your partner through a rough time, remember to give yourself a break, mentally and physically. You deserve it. You're doing a brilliant job.

25

Nothing is Impossible

I refuse to let my disability define me. Disabled people should never be underestimated or ruled out.

One of my all-time heroes is Stephen Hawking, the theoretical physicist famous for writing *A Brief History of Time*. He's also famous for having made his biggest scientific breakthroughs while paralysed by an early onset form of motor neurone disease. When Hawking first went to Cambridge University – where I would study years later – he was able-bodied. He was diagnosed with motor neurone disease in 1963, aged only twenty-one, and given a life expectancy of just two years. He beat that expectation by more than half a century. In the meantime, his scientific research garnered him a list of awards as long as your arm. He made theoretical physics accessible to the masses with his books *A Brief History of Time*, *The Theory of Everything* and *The Grand Design*. He married twice and had three children.

I met Hawking for the first time before I became blind, while I was still a student at Cambridge. His energy was palpable. You could feel it. He focused his mind and achieved everything he wanted to by pushing the boundaries. He just kept going. He did not let his disability hold him back in any way. When I lost my sight, Hawking became my role model. I decided that I too would find that inner strength. Like him, I would achieve everything I had hoped to before I lost my sight.

Dave – my friend and mentor at Guide Dogs – once described it like this: the human brain operates at 50kW. When you have a disability, you just have to operate at 500kW to get the same effect. Hawking ran on a higher voltage than most of the people around him. That was what I was going to have to do.

I'd always had big dreams – I'd learned to fly, I'd become a doctor, I'd met and married the woman of my dreams. Why should blindness stop me achieving everything I'd planned? I had Seema, I had Kika and I had little Abhi. I'd gone back to work and I'd pushed myself physically in ways I never would have thought possible.

As a guest of the Calvert Trust in Exmoor, I'd tried accessible rock climbing, abseiling, cycling and kayaking. It was incredible for my self-confidence to do activities that I had previously thought were off-limits to me. I'd had an enormous fear of being in water since losing my sight; I don't go swimming any more because of it. So for me to be out on open water in a kayak was a big deal. Every day I was pushing the boundaries of what I'd believed possible. Every day I was getting closer to my dream life, ticking all the boxes. But what I had always wanted to do was drive a car at break-neck speed around a professional racetrack . . .

Having learned to drive at the age of fourteen, three years before I was even old enough to get a provisional licence, I was always fascinated by cars, bikes and planes – anything that would enable me to go fast and feel free with, preferably, an added element of risk. I loved to watch *Top Gear*, especially the 'Star in a Reasonably Fast Car' section of the show where a celebrity was invited to race around a track. I'd often wondered if I could do better than the celebs. Maybe I could even do better than The Stig?

But when I lost my sight, of course, I lost the ability to drive too. It was one of the most frustrating and upsetting losses I incurred on that terrible day, not least because Seema and I had only recently bought a new car. And I loved that car. At weekends I could spend four or five hours at a time just cleaning and polishing its perfect shiny paintwork. It was my way of switching off after a hard working week.

Fortunately, Seema can drive, though when we first met that wasn't the case. Before we got married, I made her promise me she would learn so we could take it in turns when we went out to socialize. When Seema got her driving licence, it was a happy day in the Patel household, and these days Seema is a very confident driver. She isn't afraid of London traffic or of taking long trips on the motorway. But she still doesn't enjoy driving like I used to. She can take it or leave it.

I missed driving so much. Just being able to pick up my car keys and go had meant so much to me. I'd always wondered if I would ever sit in the driving seat again. But it was impossible. Of course it was. If you can't see, you can't drive, right? You've got to be able to see the road and the other cars. End of. When you're blind, you're on the bus. But that didn't stop me wishing it could be otherwise.

Since starting my work as a disability advocate, I've been offered the opportunity to do a great many things I might not otherwise have done. I've given speeches in front of thousands of people, I've been to Parliament and Downing Street. I've been interviewed on radio and television. I've met politicians and celebrities. I've been given the chance to make a real difference. I never take any of the opportunities I've been given for granted, but when Toyota offered to make it possible for me to drive again, I thought I must really be dreaming.

Toyota – the Japanese car company – is a big supporter of Guide Dogs. In March 2018, Toyota GB and Guide Dogs announced the launch of a two-year partnership during which Toyota would pay for the training of four new guide dog puppies. It was a generous offer. The training costs for each dog are more than £50,000. To mark the partnership, staff at Toyota named three of the four pups – Else, Genchi and Poppy. A fourth puppy, Banjo, was named after a social media campaign to choose a suitable name.

Toyota is also a big sponsor of the Paralympics. Their campaign around the latest games had the strapline 'Start Your Impossible'. So when Scott Brownlee, the head of PR for Toyota, started following me on Twitter, I took the opportunity to send him a message regarding his company's promise. *I* wanted to achieve the impossible. Could Toyota help me get behind the wheel again? Even if it was only in the car park?

It was a cheeky request and I didn't honestly expect anything to come of it, but Scott replied within a couple of hours. His response was, 'Leave it with me.'

Within a few days, Scott had arranged a conference call with key people from his PR and marketing team and me. I told them that while having Kika had given me back a great deal of independence, I still missed being able to pick up my car keys and go. Was there any way I could feel that sense of freedom again? The Toyota team thought there might be.

A few months after that conference call, Scott phoned me again with a date. It was a Tuesday in May. Could I be at an aerodrome near Oxford for 10 a.m.? The runway at the aerodrome had been used in the filming of *The Fast and the Furious*. It was also the home base of U Drive, a company that provided driving experiences in supercars like Ferraris and Lamborghinis. As it happened, they provided driving experiences for the visually impaired too. Scott had been talking to the company's owner, who thought that one of their specialist driving instructors – a former rally driver named Mark Watkins – could be the man to help me get back behind the wheel.

'Are you up for it?' Scott asked. You bet I was!

Seeing as bare-faced cheek had already got me so far, I asked if I could bring along a mate: Dave, my friend from Guide Dogs. Having been visually impaired since birth, Dave had never been able to drive, but I knew that getting behind the wheel of a car was definitely on his wish list. Scott said Toyota would be glad to help us both. When I phoned Dave to let him know, he couldn't believe it. His excitement fuelled mine. We were like a couple of schoolkids looking forward to the end-of-term trip.

When I told Seema that Toyota was offering me the chance to get back behind the wheel, she thought I was pulling her leg. How on earth could they make it happen? Were they talking about putting me into a driving simulator? That would make sense. I couldn't hurt myself in a simulator.

'No. Where's the fun in that?' I asked. 'They're putting me in a real car.'

Seema took a deep breath. I could tell it worried her. But no matter how crazy the whole idea was, of course she already knew I was going to go through with it.

The day arrived. Since Dave and I would be travelling to Oxfordshire from different parts of London, we made a plan to meet at a service station ten miles from the aerodrome and do the last part of the trip together. It was a family day out for us Patels. Seema, Abhi and Kika were all with me. Dave was accompanied that day by his close friend and PA Mel, and, naturally, Chad his guide dog.

We arrived bang on time. Nothing could have compelled us to be late for this experience. Mark, the instructor, was already waiting for us, as was Scott. Toyota had sent along two cars: a Yaris hybrid and a Toyota GT86. A camera crew was also there to record our adventures.

Chad and Kika stayed with Seema and Abhi, who was in his element having two dogs to play with, while Dave and I followed Mark to the cars. We started with a safety briefing. Mark laid down the parameters for the day ahead. The school trip atmosphere continued, with Dave and me winding each other up to fever pitch. Which of us would be the faster driver? I humoured Dave but I was already pretty sure it would be me.

The first car we tried was the Yaris. Mark walked me around the car so that I could get a sense of how big it was, then I got into the driver's seat while Mark talked me through the controls from the passenger side. I had a good reference of where things would be from the driver's seat given that I was able to drive before losing my sight. It was familiar enough that I didn't have to worry about any of the ancillary controls – I just needed to know where the brake and accelerator were. The car was automatic so I didn't need to be able to find the gears. I wasn't wearing a helmet because, as far as Mark was concerned, we weren't going to be driving terribly fast. I would need time to respond to his instructions. 'I'll count you down before each turn,' Mark told me.

Mark didn't sound unduly concerned about the challenge ahead, but he had to trust me to do exactly as he asked. With no dual controls such as you get in a learner car, the only thing he could do to save the situation if I messed up was pull on the handbrake. I told him he was a brave guy.

The Yaris was electric. It turned on at the touch of a button. I was disappointed not to hear the familiar sound of a petrol engine roaring into life, but all the same I was excited to be driving at last five years after going blind.

I pressed down on the accelerator and we set off at a snail's pace to do my first circuit of the airfield. I wasn't nervous. After so many years of blindness, I was well used to being guided and could quickly turn oral instructions into a 3D image in my head. Mark had done a good job of describing the course before we set off and his instructions were clear. In many ways, I think it was easier for me to trust him because I didn't have any sight at all and I couldn't make my own judgement. I had to use his.

For the next fifteen to twenty minutes, Mark and I took the car around the block again and again. As I gained confidence I got a little faster. It was hard, though, for me to know *how* fast. Since the car was automatic *and* electric, I couldn't feel or hear any changes in the engine that might give me a clue. But it was great to be behind the wheel again. When Dave returned from his own first circuit in the Yaris, I could hear how excited he was too.

'How amazing was that?' he said breathlessly. 'I can't wait to do it again.'

We broke for lunch. While we were eating, a member of the Toyota team took Mark away for a private discussion regarding my progress in the car. How did he think I was getting on? Fortunately for me, Mark agreed with my own assessment that I was ready to drive the GT86.

The Toyota GT86 is the two-door, rear-wheel-drive car used in the 'Star in a Reasonably Fast Car' segment of BBC's *Top Gear*. The GT86 I would be driving was exactly the same as the *Top Gear* car, with no dual controls. Unlike the Yaris, it was a manual with a petrol engine. I knew it would be an entirely different experience. I couldn't wait.

After lunch, Mark took me around the GT86 just as he'd taken me around the Yaris, helping me to get a sense of its size. Then I settled into the driver's seat and, once again, Mark ran through the controls. As I turned the car on and I felt the revs, a smile spread across my face.

'Ready?' Mark asked.

I was ready.

Immediately, I knew I'd be able to drive this new car far better and far faster than the Yaris. Ultimately, it was quite simple. Like a rally driver on a cross-country course, all I had to do was do exactly as my co-driver commanded – turning the wheel, cranking through the gears and braking when he told me to. I didn't actually need to be able to see at all.

Mark had started out by giving me a countdown as we approached each turn, but after a while he asked, 'Would you be comfortable with me saying ninety left or ninety right?' I told him that I would be.

With these new more precise directions, I was able to speed up. Soon we were doing eighty miles an hour, then eighty-five, then ninety . . . This was more like it!

'Want to do a doughnut?' Mark asked.

You bet I did.

I was in the car for a couple of hours that afternoon. Scott from Toyota was delighted by the footage the team captured that day. Unbeknown to us, it convinced him that I was capable of much more than he had anticipated and now he wanted to give me the chance to drive the 'Reasonably Fast Car' around the *Top Gear* track for real. Scott pulled in his A-team from DMS media – Dan and Elliot.

In the last week of October 2018, Elliot called. He told me, 'Amit, you need Seema to measure you for a race suit.'

I knew at once what that meant. He was asking whether I wanted to go driving again: this time in the actual *Top Gear* car on the actual *Top Gear* racetrack.

It was all very hush hush. The night before the big day, Kika and I went to stay with Mum and Dad in Guildford. The following morning they drove us to Dunsfold Aerodrome – the airfield where *Top Gear* is filmed – which is just ten miles away from where they live. Dunsfold is a commercial airport, still very much in use. Iconic planes line the runway.

When we arrived, the Toyota team, the media team, Mark, my navigator, and the emergency services were already in place. Mark told me he had driven in from Gloucestershire to be there, leaving at five in the morning to do the more than three-hour drive.

In the McLaren suite – which was basically an expensive shed with a kitchen and lounge – I changed into my new race suit. Mum and Dad looked after Kika while I followed Mark down onto the track where the car was waiting.

A mechanic was hovering nervously. He was there to make sure that the Toyota was spotless at the beginning of each shoot. This car was his baby. He made a point of telling me that he didn't have any spare parts.

It was a cold, wet morning and Mark had yet to test the car's capabilities. He took it out on his own to get an idea of the track. When he returned, he told me that the track was 'wet, wet'.

'But not Wet, Wet, Wet,' I joked.

Later, Mark told me that after returning from that test lap, he'd been pulled to one side by the Toyota crew and instructed that he must not push me. He had to let me lead and stick to the speed with which I was comfortable.

I hit three minutes on my second go around the track.

That first day, Mark and I spent six hours in the car, getting to know the track. I memorized each and every turn. I spun the car once, when I hit the grass verge, narrowly missing a runway light. As soon as I felt myself losing control, everything I'd learned for the advanced driving test I took as an A&E doctor kicked in and I safely brought the car to a stop. I expected Mark to be concerned but he merely said, 'You need to know where your limit is.' He was perfectly calm about it.

Though I was driving far faster than anyone in the crew had expected, I was frustrated that I wasn't getting the kind of times I knew the celebrities on *Top Gear* had achieved. When I expressed my frustration, Mark told me it was because we were taking the official line. We weren't cutting any corners, as the celebrities often did. So I asked one of the crew members to google some *Top Gear* videos on YouTube and describe to me where the shortcuts were. Everyone was surprised at how seriously I was taking it. I knew that opportunities like this didn't come along every day. I wanted to make the most of it.

That night, the whole team stayed at a hotel near the airfield. Mark and I were the last to go to bed. We went over our strategy for the next day again and again, visualizing the track in minute detail. As we said goodnight, Mark said, 'I think we can do one minute fifty-five.'

I told him, 'I think we can do one forty-five.'

The following day was dry but the track was still damp. The emergency team did a few circuits of the track to disperse the worst of the water. We knew we wouldn't have as much track time that day because there were interviews to be recorded too. We also had to keep the runway clear for a number of planes that were due to land or take off.

As soon as we were able, Mark and I started to warm up the car. We took a couple of slow laps before bringing the car up to a speed of 120 miles an hour. Then, suddenly, the runway lights came on to warn us a plane was about to land. It was not expected. We took the car off the runway at once.

After lunch, I filmed my interview at the top of the runway

and spoke quite emotionally about my sight loss journey. Standing there on the runway, cameras pointed at me, it seemed incredible that I had come this far. As soon as we got back in the car and got started the runway lights came on again. It happened three times in two hours. It was deeply frustrating since it took so long to set up again each time, but I understood our safety was the most important thing.

How many people watch those celebs going around the *Top Gear* test track and think, *I could do better*? I'd been given the chance to *prove* I could do better. I was determined I would not mess up. I wanted to do the best I could for so many reasons. I wanted to do my best for Abhi and Seema. I didn't want to let down the team either.

I told the cameras during my interview that the only reason I was standing there at all was because of Seema. Our connection had kept me going through the very worst of times. As I talked about her unwavering love and support, I started to cry. I needed that cry.

Seema didn't see the interview but she was there to see me drive and cheer me on. Kika was by her side and so was Abhi. He was at the age when he was just beginning to be interested in cars, trains and planes. Though I have to admit that he was more interested in the red fire truck than the red car that his daddy was driving.

As the all-important timed lap, the lap that would count for posterity, approached, I began to feel nervous. Could I do it? Could I beat the time I'd set in my head?

'We'd really appreciate it if you didn't total this car,' said one of the team from Toyota as they completed their final checks. Then the support team moved out of the way and it was just Mark and me again. I pressed the start button and the engine came to life. I pressed my foot down on the accelerator and heard a reassuring roar as I felt the power travel through my body.

'Are you ready?' Mark asked me.

I gave him a nod and pushed the pedal to the metal. We were off.

We did two practice laps. On the first, I didn't turn left fast enough at the end of the straight. The second was better and faster. On the final lap, the timed lap, I nearly lost it on a bend. We estimated that I dropped three seconds correcting that mistake. Then the film crew's camera drone came in and swooped in front of the car. Mark told me that he just closed his eyes and waited for the collision. But these guys knew what they were doing. The drone missed us, whooshing over the car in true Hollywood style, and we finished the lap.

'How fast?' was all I wanted to know as I took off my helmet. 'How fast? How did I do?'

It was one of the most amazing days of my life. Seema tells me you can see from the footage that I'm having a wonderful time. When I step from the car, I'm grinning from ear to ear.

To feel the accelerator pedal beneath my foot again, to turn the wheel and feel the car instantly respond, to have the sensation of speed pressing me back into my seat and know that I was the one in ultimate control . . . It was the most incredible feeling. I felt like the kid who learned to drive on the old airfield again. The old Amit, the one who would do anything for an adrenalin rush, was still there inside me.

As I stepped from the car, with my legs slightly shaky from all the excitement and adrenalin, Seema brought Abhi and

Kika over to greet me. They were both so pleased to see me – though Abhi was possibly more excited about getting closer to the airfield's fire engine – and both Abhi and Kika had a go at wearing my helmet.

So, how did I do? It turns out I did pretty well. I achieved a top speed around the track of one minute forty-six seconds. That would have put me pretty close to the top of the *Top Gear* celebrity leader board. I was right behind Chris Hoy. I beat Tiny Tempah and David Tennant. I think if I'd had just one more go, I'd have smashed through a couple of records. Stig, eat your heart out.

Back at home that night, I reflected on all the things I'd done since the day I lost my sight.

There have been some incredibly heartbreakingly difficult times, but that day on the racetrack was a real high and it made me more confident than ever that, like Stephen Hawking, I could still live my dream life. The only limit was my own imagination.

Next on my agenda is to persuade a friendly airline to let me loose in the cockpit of a plane . . .

Epilogue

Since I began writing this book, life in the Patel household has been busier than ever. I've been speaking all over the country – and the continent – in my role as a campaigner and accessibility consultant. Naturally, Kika has been with me and her hard work has not gone unrecognized. In November 2018, Kika won 'Assistance Animal of the Year' at the inaugural Animal Star Awards. This year I'll be going back to judge the category, with a little help from Kika, of course!

We've taken part in some more great fundraising events in 2019. In May, I joined the RNIB's Double Dash with my running partner Emily Marr. It's a race in which pairs of runners are attached at the wrist for a five-kilometre run. Unfortunately, it didn't go quite as well as I hoped. I injured my knee in training and, though I did my best to keep going through the excruciating pain on race day, I didn't make it to the finish line. In fact, I had to be stretchered off and taken to A&E. I ended up spending the night in hospital.

In June, as promised, Kika and I partnered with the Eden Project again and hosted The Big Lunch on our own street. In preparation, I was asked by the National Lottery to tell the story of my sight loss and how my community had helped me at a difficult time. This resulted in my being filmed in a water tank to bring to life my own description of my sight loss – that sensation of being in a deep pool. Filming this segment ended up being more than just an immersive experience: it was cathartic too. Even during the long drive to the studio with Kelvin the director and his film crew I was still in two minds as to whether it was something I could do, especially knowing that it would be just me in the water with no breathing apparatus. But eventually I found myself at the bottom of a twelve-foot tank wearing pyjamas and a dressing gown and thankfully a crew member jumped in to act as my lifeguard. It was a tough day but when I got out of the tank, I felt elated.

The street party was a fantastic success. I had flyered all the neighbouring streets but was still petrified that no one would show up on the day. As it happened, the weather was brilliant and the turnout was huge, turning neighbours who were just acquaintances into proper friends. Kika gained a new fan in Jean, who has lived in the house opposite ours for fifty years.

For the party, we covered the street with bunting. When it was over, we left some of it up for another celebration which happened just a couple of weeks later. You see, the really big news of 2019 was the arrival of Team Patel's newest member.

In the middle of June, Anoushka, a baby sister for Abhi and Kika, was born. Anoushka arrived in a hurry, earlier than expected, and caught us all a little off-guard given that we were still in the middle of having the house renovated. There was no floor downstairs, no useable kitchen and there were still holes in walls.

Seema went into labour late in the evening. I had to wake

Abhi up so that we could take him to the hospital with us. Not an ideal situation, but fate was on our side. When the taxi arrived to take us to the hospital, the driver recognized me immediately. He was the same gentleman who had driven us to the hospital almost three years earlier when Abhi was born. We all piled into his car once more, this time with a sleepy Abhi holding on to me tightly. Kika sat patiently by my feet. The familiar theme continued on arrival at the hospital, where we were shown to the same room in the birth centre that we'd been in with Abhi, with the same midwife. Daisy delivered both our babies – the second in record time. Kika barely had a moment to make herself comfortable before she was able to get a sniff of her new baby sister. During our brief stint in the birth centre, Kika took it upon herself to look after Abhi, presumably so that I could concentrate on Seema. Not only did Kika help to comfort Abhi but in turn kept us all calm too.

Anoushka's arrival has brought some perspective to our crazy busy lives and we can't wait to get to know her better. Now I really am outnumbered!

What a journey it's been. Blindness is always there, it's always going to be in my life, but I no longer wake up in the morning thinking, *Oh my goodness, I'm blind, what do I do?* I just get on with it. It's easy to say that now, but believe me, five years ago it wasn't.

I have an amazing wife who put her arms around me and gave me hugs when I most needed it. Seema has been with me every step of the way. She gave me the motivation and the love that got me from my lowest ebb to where I am now. It's made us who we are today.

We have a wonderful young son and daughter. In my head, I can see the smiles on their faces. I'm hoping that when they're older, they'll be proud of what their dad's achieved. I don't want them to ever think, *Daddy's not able to do this.* I want them to grow up knowing that being blind won't stop me from achieving things. I hope it will encourage them to follow their wildest dreams too.

In the meantime, the lovely, ordinary life we live today is due in no small part to the fifth member of our happy family: Kika. As I write this, she is snoring on her bed in the corner of the room, her big paws twitching as she dreams of chasing squirrels in the park. She likes to be nearby as I work. From time to time, she gets up, wanders over and puts her heavy head on my knee to remind me she's still there. I stroke her floppy ears, as soft as velvet, and listen to her happy snuffles. She is not just my guide dog, she's my dear friend.

She keeps me safe. She gives me confidence. She knows how to comfort me when I'm having a rough day. Kika has changed my life beyond recognition, returning me to a level of independence I had thought lost forever when I went blind. I always believed that everything happens for a reason, so perhaps it's no coincidence that I lost my sight in November 2013 and that Kika was born in November 2013 as well.

I live a wonderfully ordinary life thanks to one extraordinary dog. Kika has opened up the world to me again. She's made what once seemed impossible possible. Together with Seema, Abhi and Anoushka, Kika makes life a big new adventure every day. We do it differently but we do it together, and that's what it's all about.

Ask Amit

Sometimes people are nervous about talking to me. They worry that they can't use certain terms. It's common for me to say things like, 'It's nice to see you', 'I see what you mean' or 'if you look at it like that', when I'm not actually referring to *seeing* something in a visual sense. Often part way through a conversation, someone will apologize for having used that sort of visual language. I don't mind. I don't consider it insensitive at all. I think we have to pick our battles and stopping people from using perfectly natural turns of phrase because they might exclude the visually impaired is not a battle I choose to fight. Or even believe should be a battle at all.

People also worry how to refer to blindness. What is the difference between being 'visually impaired' and being 'blind'? For me, blindness refers to a world of darkness while visual impairment is a spectrum. When I'm talking about myself, I use the term 'blind', though someone who is officially registered severely sight impaired (blind) might have residual sight.

And then people worry that they might ask the wrong sort of question. Children are much less scared to ask – they're not afraid of offending anyone – but I want everyone I meet, young or old, to feel able to ask me all the questions they have about visual impairment so that I can demystify the experience for them. We're only afraid of what we don't understand. If I can help people to understand blindness and the issues that arise from it, then I am happy to answer the stupidest questions you've got. And I bet they're not really stupid questions at all. Here are some of the things I'm most commonly asked.

Why don't you look blind?

This one always puzzles me. What is a blind person supposed to look like? Am I supposed to look like I got dressed in the dark? As I've explained, the way I dress has always been important to me and I like to dress well.

Or perhaps when people say I don't look blind, what they really mean is that my eyes somehow don't look as 'unseeing' as they imagine they should. That might be because I used to have sight, so my natural instinct is to orientate my gaze towards the voice of whoever is talking to me, which I suppose could give the impression that I am 'looking' at them. The blind person stereotype of dark glasses exists because many people with visual impairments find that light hurts their eyes. That goes for me too. My eyes constantly feel like they've had chilli powder rubbed into them and the glasses help manage the pain. A lot of the time my eyes are completely bloodshot and inflamed – dark glasses hide this from the public so that they don't get freaked out.

I've seen you using a mobile phone – how does that work?

I personally use an iPhone because they have accessibility software hard-wired in. What does that mean? The phone essentially reads out what is on the screen, which then allows me to navigate with swipes and taps, without needing to see it. With practice it becomes second nature but always seems to baffle people around me because there's nothing to see on the screen.

When it comes to taking photos I just point and shoot. Sometimes all I capture are selfies when the camera is facing the wrong way but on occasion I do manage to get a decent shot.

There are plenty of apps out there for the visually impaired that use artificial intelligence to identify objects using the phone's camera and can even read handwritten text, such as on a birthday card or letter.

Do I want to know what you look like?

On a couple of occasions, people have asked me whether I'd like to feel their face to get a sense of what they 'look' like. At first, I wondered where the question was coming from, but then someone reminded me of the 1980s Lionel Richie song 'Hello'. In the video that accompanies the song, Richie plays an acting teacher in the throes of unrequited love for a blind student. He's convinced his feelings are unreciprocated until he discovers that she's been busy making a sculpture of his head in clay. She feels his face in order to 'see' him.

Anyway, the answer to that question is, 'No, I don't want to feel your face.' Seriously. Please don't ask. I really don't want to be sticking my fingers up a new acquaintance's nose to get to know them better. A verbal description will do just fine, thanks.

Have your other senses heightened since you lost your sight?

I don't think my other senses have really increased in sensitivity, but I have learned to understand them better. For example, my hearing hasn't changed but the way I use it has. I can now filter out noise, focus my hearing on what's in front of me or listen out for particular sounds like train announcements.

Can you dream?

I do still dream visually and I occasionally talk in my sleep. When I first lost my sight I tried so hard not to forget what my loved ones looked like. Now it's only in my dreams that I remember. But that also means I have very vivid nightmares. If I've had a bad commute, it gets played out in my head overnight. My brain comes out with all the witty put-downs I wish I'd used at the time. No more Mr Nice Guy. Seema lets me talk, even if I'm keeping her awake. She knows it's important for me to let it all out.

My mind is always active. I want to do so much. I'm physically tired all the time but if I don't keep myself busy, the pain in my eyes becomes more noticeable. Even this long after losing my sight I still experience relentless pain. I've just learned to control it more effectively.

How can I help a blind person in the street?

If you see that a guide dog owner is standing still having dropped their dog's harness, it is a sign that they may need assistance, so ask them if that's the case.

If you see a visually impaired person on the street, at a station or on your travels, regardless of whether they have a guide dog, a symbol cane or a long white cane, don't always assume that they will need help. But if you want to offer help, always introduce yourself first. Don't just shout, 'Do you want help?', because in a busy environment, a visually impaired person may not realize you're talking to them. If it's busy or loud, I don't mind a light tap on my arm or shoulder to get my attention. Ask how you can help and don't be offended if they decline. Let them tell you what they need and be sure to say goodbye before you go.

What if I offend a visually impaired person by asking them if they need assistance?

You should never assume that someone wants to be guided, but it's far better to offer help than not. If you ask and receive a refusal, don't take it personally.

If a VIP does take offence, rest assured that it's not about you. We all have different personalities. We all have good days and bad days. Please don't stop offering your help if one person seems upset by the gesture. You might just make the next person's day a whole lot easier. For the record, you could never offend me by asking me if I need assistance. Even if I don't want help, knowing that people are willing to offer it gives me reassurance.

In busy areas you get something called 'diffusion of responsibility'. Even when someone is obviously struggling, everyone assumes that someone else is going to help, with the end result being that nobody does. So make sure you're the person everyone else is relying on to step up!

How should I support a VIP physically?

Ask the VIP how they want to be guided. They'll let you know.

While you're walking, you don't need to give a running commentary of everything you see. Don't bombard the VIP with information. Instead, give them the relevant information. Tell them if they're approaching a kerb, where the handrails are, if there's a door . . .

But otherwise, strike up a conversation. Ask how their day has been. Tell them your name and what you're up to. Talk to a VIP like you'd talk to anyone. Incidentally, quite often, I've found that people helping me address their conversation to Kika. I'd like to be included, please.

How should I leave the situation?

Don't just walk off without a word, as some people do. Tell the VIP that you're going before you disappear! There's nothing more embarrassing than continuing to chat to thin air. I've often been left talking to myself as I didn't realize that the person who had been helping me had left!

Can I pat your guide dog?

That depends on the context. You should never distract a working assistance animal. If the guide dog owner is holding the dog's harness, then that dog is definitely working and you should give it a little more space if you can. Please don't disturb the dog, even if it's standing still on an escalator or at a road crossing and doesn't appear to be doing much. Someone once offered Kika a crisp as we were getting close to the top of some stairs, with the result that she was distracted and I ended up tripping over her.

In other circumstances, such as if the guide dog owner is sitting on a train and the dog is resting by his or her feet, it may be OK to say hello, but always ask the owner for permission first. While guide dogs are bred for their easy-going temperaments, not all guide dogs like to be petted by strangers. Likewise, some are more protective of their owners than others. They all have different personalities.

Can I give your dog a treat?

No, you can't. Never feed a guide dog. Please don't ignore this advice and think that if you slip a guide dog a treat it won't matter because their owner can't see. Of course the dog will take whatever you offer. They can't make a decision about what's good for them. Guide dogs are well fed and their food is specially chosen to suit their weight, age and health. This ensures that they get all the vitamins and nutrients they need and also ensures consistency in their spending – their poo – so that their owner can tell straight away from their poo if something is wrong with their dog's health. They're not used to other food, not least human food, and this could upset their stomach and their spending routine. The last thing I want is Kika being caught short when we're in the office!

Some dogs also have allergies. Inadvertently feeding a guide dog something that makes it ill can cause serious problems for the dog and for the owner who may be unable to go about their daily life or get into work while their dog is recovering from a tummy upset or worse.

So if you see my Kika making eyes at you while you eat crisps or a sandwich on the train, please ignore her. She gets plenty to eat at home!

Does your guide dog do tricks?

I would have thought that making sure I get through a busy London train station safely is impressive enough, but people often ask if Kika does any tricks. She doesn't. She won't let you shake her paw. She doesn't need to.

Can guide dogs really go anywhere?

The rights of assistance dog owners were laid down in the Equality Act of 2010. They have the right to access public spaces and services such as shops, banks, hotels, restaurants, libraries and museums. Not even a butcher's shop can refuse to allow a guide dog entry, which is fortunate for us.

Guide dog owners also have the right to use taxis. It is actually against the law for a taxi or minicab driver to refuse an assistance dog owner access to his or her car, unless the driver is in possession of a certificate from a GP giving them a medical exemption. As it stands, there are just a handful of UK taxi and minicab drivers who have claimed this official exemption.

This isn't to say that guide dog owners necessarily *should* take their dogs everywhere. The dog's happiness and safety have to be taken into consideration too.

How does Kika know where to find the milk in the supermarket?

She doesn't. She's not much help at finding the BOGOF offers either. When we're at a supermarket, I ask Kika to take me to a member of staff who can help me to find what I need and tell me what else is available. Though sometimes I like to joke with my fellow customers by loudly telling Kika to 'make sure you get the blue top this time' when we're in the dairy aisle.

Likewise, if a guide dog owner asks you for directions, there's not much point crouching down to give the directions directly to the dog. Believe me, that does happen! Kika is undoubtedly very intelligent, but telling her to take the second left after the postbox isn't much use. Tell me, then *I* can tell Kika to turn left when we reach the second kerb.

How does Kika let you know you're in danger?

There is no specific guide dog signal for 'danger'. Each dog has its own way of signalling to its owner. In Kika's case, as happened on the day when we had to be picked up in a police car, she will sit on my feet. I can also tell when she's hesitating for some reason because I feel it through her harness.

What does Kika's average day look like?

If it's a nursery run day, then Kika gets up at 5.30 a.m. and, by default, that's the time I get up too. The first thing I do upon waking is groom Kika's fur. I brush her all over with a soft brush, then clean away the sleep from around her eyes. Grooming is very important. It's a bonding exercise. It also helps to get rid of the loose fur that would otherwise go all over me and everyone else who comes into contact with her (boy, does Kika shed). It allows me to feel for bites, injuries or lumps. Like many Labradors, Kika has the odd fatty lump that changes size according to how well she's feeling. It's important for me to keep an eye on those. Once a week I clean her ears.

I don't often have to bathe Kika. Her coat is kept pretty clean by the daily brushing. Labradors have a reputation for loving water. They even have slightly webbed feet that help them to swim. However, Kika is one Lab who isn't keen on taking a dip so I don't have to worry about that. At the time of writing, she hasn't had a bath for six months and then it was only because she'd rolled in some fox poo while off the lead and was stinking the whole house out.

By 5.45 a.m., with grooming time finished, I give Kika her breakfast. She eats a special guide dog formula, designed to keep her in the best of health. It's a sort of kibble. Feeding guide dogs treats is a tricky area. Because Kika is a working dog and she often has to spend long hours in strange offices, being able to regulate her bowel movements is important. Straying too far off her diet could cause disastrous accidents. That doesn't mean she never gets a healthy treat, though. Kika loves vegetables, especially carrots, cucumber and radishes.

While Kika's eating I put on coffee for me and Seema and make a babyccino – that is, frothed milk – for Abhi. Kika finishes her food and waits for my command to 'spend' – that is, pee and poo; she does it in the same place in our garden every single day so that I know where it is and it is easy for me to clean up.

Kika is normally fed an hour before we leave the house, giving her time to digest her food before we set out for the day. After another quick groom of Kika's coat, we usually leave at 7.30 a.m. to do the nursery drop-off and then head into work in the city for the day. This entails taking a train into central London and then often a Tube or bus, but most times I'd rather walk a few miles across town to get to my meetings. Where it's just as easy to walk as take public transport, I do that so that both Kika and I get some exercise. Kika loves the hustle and bustle of the city; she thrives on working in busy environments and enjoys the challenge of navigating difficult places. She's a proper city dog in that sense and can hold her own on the Tube. She can even find me a coffee shop when I really need it!

When we get back home, Kika has her second meal of the day and we have the same spending routine as in the morning. Now she's off the harness, she's the family pet again. She plays with Abhi, cuddles up to Seema for a while, then usually falls asleep while I'm reading Abhi a story.

Kika sees a vet every three months to make sure she's in tip-top condition. One of the things we have to watch is her weight. If Kika isn't working as much as she needs to, she quickly puts on the pounds. I can tell when I'm putting on her harness whether she's up or down from her ideal weight. Every three years, Kika gets a rabies jab for her pet passport.

What happens when a guide dog needs to go to the loo?

Guide dogs are trained to spend on command so that their owners can be relatively sure they won't need to nip out in the middle of a meeting for a doggy loo break. City-based guide dogs usually poo a couple of times a day and they are trained to go in a drain when they need to.

Kika has a 'spending area' in the garden at home. If, while we're out, Kika wants to pee, she just squats and gets on with it. If she wants to do anything else, she gives her harness a little shake, and I stop. She takes two steps forward and does her business. I then take a poo bag and aim for where I think the poo has landed.

Unlike other dog owners, guide dog owners are not obliged to pick up after their dogs – we're exempt – but I think it's only good manners to do what I can to clean up after Kika. I've learned over time to buy only the thickest poo bags available. One good thing is that poo bags can double as nappy bags. There have been occasions when I've been out with Abhi and have been caught short on the nappy bag front. However, my advice is never, ever try to use a nappy bag as a poo bag. Trust me, it doesn't work that way round. Not with my Kika anyway!

What are the rules of guide dog ownership?

Guide dogs are bred and specially trained for their jobs. Each dog represents an enormous investment in terms of training time, volunteer hours and financial cost. All to make a person's daily life easier. That life-changing dog also means the owner taking on a full-time responsibility – for the health and welfare of the dog as well as their training, so that they can continue to work and keep their owner safe.

That means making sure they have their regular flea treatments and worming tablets, alongside regular check-ups with the vet. It also means making sure that you don't put the dog's health at risk. I avoid taking Kika with me to concerts and events with loud noises as it would be distressing for her. Fireworks displays are the same as they can be stressful for dogs.

The other key rule is that guide dog owners are not allowed to be drunk in charge of a guide dog, for obvious reasons.

What are the practicalities of travelling with a guide dog?

As Kika is a registered assistance dog, she is allowed to accompany me to all public places and can also travel with me when I go abroad. To enable her to do so, she has an EU pet passport, issued after a series of vaccinations and checks. The pet passport includes the dog's details, microchip number, lists and dates of vaccinations and things like tapeworm treatments. There's a photo too. The first thing that you see when you open Kika's pet passport is her grinning face staring back at you – luckily for her, the human passport rules about not smiling don't apply to dogs!

The onus is always on the guide dog owner to ensure all the relevant paperwork is in place and checks are done before travelling – having a vaccination out of date by a matter of minutes could be enough to have your dog quarantined at home or in a foreign country. Additionally, every country, even within the EU, has slightly different rules and arrangements regarding entry notification and exit requirements for assistance animals. The general rule for coming back into the UK is that assistance dogs need to be administered a worming tablet by a registered vet 120 to 24 hours before arrival back into the country. This treatment needs to be written up and stamped in the pet passport and the relevant UK authority advised of the travel both before departure and once the treatment has been administered so they can prepare the arrival paperwork.

If we're flying, when the plane lands back in the UK, we're the last to leave the aircraft as the animal air care team come on board to check Kika's microchip (to make sure she is who her passport says she is), double-check her pet passport and issue her landing clearance letter. Only then can we disembark and clear customs.

Alongside this, different airlines have different rules about booking a flight with an assistance dog. Most, if not all, have limits as to how many assistance dogs they can have on each flight. Some let you book the flight and then inform them about the dog. Other airlines require you to speak to them in person before you can book a trip with an assistance dog.

Most people see a good deal on a holiday or flight and a couple of clicks later, it's all booked. It's not so simple for us. Firstly we need to consider if it's a Kika-friendly destination. By that, I don't mean dog-loving, but that we have to think about the temperature, flight time, the airline and whether there are quarantine requirements in place (this means that Asia and most long-haul, exotic destinations are off-limits if we want to take Kika with us).

We've lost out on many a great holiday deal as we were

unable to book an assistance dog place online. By the time we got through to someone on the phone, who then had to clear with a third person who always seemed to be on holiday whether there was capacity to take an assistance dog on the flight, the holiday was no longer available. Fair? I don't think so. Are we used to this happening? Sadly, yes.

At what age do guide dogs retire?

The average guide dog works with its owner for eight or nine years. Since they're usually around two years old when they begin their working lives, that means that most guide dogs retire at the age of ten or eleven. The Guide Dogs for the Blind Association liaises closely with owners throughout a dog's career to determine the right moment to retire for that particular dog. Monitoring is stepped up as a guide dog reaches eight. It's not just a dog's health that might begin to make working difficult. Occasionally a dog just gets fed up of working, as we humans do.

Do guide dogs stay with their owners after they retire?

That depends. If the guide dog owner is able to accommodate all the dog's needs post-retirement then of course the dog can remain in the family. However, most guide dogs find it difficult when their owner begins training with a new guide dog. The original dog – used to working and being out with his or her owner every day – gets bored and can become unhappy being left at home. In that situation, it's better for the old dog to go to a new home where it will get plenty of stimulation and fuss again.

Guide dog owners are allowed to nominate new owners for their retired dogs. Many end up going to live with the people who were involved in their training. Guide Dogs also has an official rehoming programme which places retired dogs with members of the public who want to adopt them. There's quite a waiting list.

There are, of course, many advantages to rehoming a retired guide dog. You won't have to train them to walk to heel or sit at the kerb. However, what people applying to rehome retired guide dogs need to remember is that when a guide dog is no longer working, the access rights it had as an assistance dog no longer apply and its status returns to that of the average pet pooch, meaning you can't take it into shops or restaurants.

There are also the usual medical problems associated with taking on an older dog, though Guide Dogs will help new owners to cover the costs of any pre-existing conditions such as arthritis.

What will happen when Kika retires?

When Kika retires – which is still some way off – she will be going to live with my parents in Guildford. Because Seema and I both have busy careers, it's likely that Kika would get very bored being stuck at home while a new dog accompanies me on my commute. We've seen how fed up she gets when I'm ill and can't take her out. We think it would be cruel for her to be relegated to the sidelines while she sees another dog take her place.

Kika already spends 'holidays' with Mum and Dad and thoroughly enjoys her time with them. For their part, they are looking forward to having Kika full-time. I'm grateful that this means Kika will still be very much in our lives. She's absolutely part of our family and we wouldn't have it any other way.

If a new operation might be able to restore your sight, would you go for it?

Sometimes people ask if I would put myself through any more procedures in the hope of regaining my sight. The fact is that it's not just that my corneas aren't working any more. Since the blood vessels at the back of my eyes were ruptured, light is bounced onto my retina but the optic nerve doesn't pass the signals on.

When it comes to surgical procedures, I've been the guinea pig too many times. I can't imagine dashing across the Atlantic to see another doctor with another crazy plan. I'm no longer young enough to bounce back. Having created a life in which I can navigate the sighted world relatively confidently, I feel I've got too much to lose now. It's taken too long to get to this stage. I didn't think I'd get here, but I'm happy where I am.

Acknowledgements

There are so many people I need to thank, both for helping to make this book happen and for the enormous roles they have played in my life and getting me through the tough times.

To my wife Seema: losing my sight didn't just affect me but equally you too, and instead of taking the easy way out you enveloped me in your love. You stood strong by my side, helping me to find myself again; you never once gave up on what we had. Your love, patience and encouragement are the reason I am truly happy. You are the single best person I know, and I'm truly blessed to be your husband.

To my parents, for having strength when I didn't. It's only now that I've become a father that I can come close to imagining how hard it must have been for you to see your son suffer so badly. But I also understand so much more why you were so determined to move the earth to help me. I love you both dearly – thank you for everything you've done for me.

To Mital and Kirsty, whose quiet, unwavering support has been there throughout, regardless of what was going on in all of our lives. Thank you so much.

Pradip kaka, Rita kaki, Veer and Jay, you took care of me when I was weak, and I'll always be grateful for your support during one of the most stressful times in my life.

This book certainly wouldn't have been possible without Lauren Gardner, my brilliant literary agent, who had to work doubly hard to convince me that people would even be interested in hearing my story. I can't thank you enough for your help and support throughout the book-writing process; it was your vision that got us here and now you won't be able to get rid of us!

My buddy Dave Kent: who would have thought five years ago that we would have made such a great double act? Without you, I would never have even considered a guide dog. Meeting you really did change my life forever, for the better. I can't thank you enough.

To Scott Brownlee and the team at Toyota, who took it upon themselves to make this ordinary blind guy's dream come true. You gave me an experience that I will cherish for the rest of my life – thank you so much. And remember, I'm always here if you need a test driver.

To Mark Watkins, my co-pilot: you are one crazy man, but that's what makes you so special. Thanks for seeing the potential in me and having my back. There's nobody else I would want by my side when I'm doing 120 miles an hour down a runway. Nürburgring here we come!

To my friend and colleague Sasha Scott, whose unswerving belief in me has helped me to rebuild my self-confidence. Thank you for being there, for believing in me and for giving me a chance.

An enormous thank you goes to my wonderful editor

Acknowledgements

Charlotte Wright and the entire team at Pan Macmillan for taking a leap of faith on me and my story.

Writing a book about the story of my life was a surreal process and I couldn't have done it without the support of my writing partner in crime Chris Manby. Thank you for helping me tell my story.

To all of you who have followed mine and Kika's adventures on Twitter over the years, the world is a better place for all the positivity, love and support that you've shown. Thank you.

And to you, my reader, thank you for picking up this book. I hope that my story has shown you that even in the darkest of times there's always a ray of light to be found. It may not come easy, but regardless of what you might be going through, I hope my journey inspires you to be brave, be strong and ask for help. Remember, you don't have to do it alone.

Resources

When I was going through a tough time, these organizations gave me help and support. If you find yourself in a similar situation, or just need someone to talk to, then perhaps they can help you too.

The Guide Dogs for the Blind Association

Guide Dogs offers a range of services for blind and partially sighted people. These, of course, include guide dogs, but it also offers a sighted guiding service called My Guide as well as supporting children and their families through sight loss.

www.guidedogs.org.uk

The Royal National Institute of Blind People

The RNIB takes a stand against exclusion, inequality and isolation to create a world without barriers for people with sight loss. The help the RNIB provides can be anything from practical and emotional support, campaigning for

change, reading services and a range of products in its
online shop.

www.rnib.org.uk

The Thomas Pocklington Trust

The TPT is a national charity dedicated to delivering positive
change for blind and partially sighted people, wherever they are
in their sight loss journey. They provide support on living with
sight loss, seeking employment and when entering education.

www.pocklington-trust.org.uk

Metro Blind Sport

Metro is a London-based charity that aims to open up sport
for all visually impaired people, regardless of age or sporting
ability. They offer activities including archery, tennis, cricket
and horse-riding, among others.

www.metroblindsport.org

Galloway's Society for the Blind

Galloway's is a leading local sight loss charity helping those
in Lancashire and Sefton. It provides practical and emotional

support, ranging from advice about equipment and technology to running social and activity groups.

www.galloways.org.uk

Henshaws

Henshaws is a northern charity helping those with sight loss and other disabilities to enjoy an independent and fulfilling life. They offer support and training to enable people and their families to build skills and confidence and help each other.

www.henshaws.org.uk

The National Eye Research Centre

The National Eye Research Centre funds research across the UK to find the causes of eye disease and to develop new prevention methods and more effective treatments for all eye diseases in both children and adults.

www.nercuk.org

Esme's Umbrella

Esme's Umbrella is a charity campaigning to build greater awareness and understanding of Charles Bonnet Syndrome.

It provides information about CBS itself and offers comfort and practical advice to those with the condition, as well as keeping up with the latest research and sharing new medical discoveries.

www.charlesbonnetsyndrome.uk

Scope

Scope is a disability equality charity in England and Wales providing practical information and emotional support, as well as campaigning for a fairer society. Scope has a free disability helpline, which is open Monday to Friday, 8 a.m. to 8 p.m., and Saturday and Sunday, 10 a.m. to 6 p.m.: 0808 800 3333.

www.scope.org.uk

The Calvert Trust

The Calvert Trust helps disabled adults and children to enjoy outdoor adventure in the countryside, offering a range of activities and appropriate accommodation.

www.calvert-trust.org.uk